STUDENT UNIT

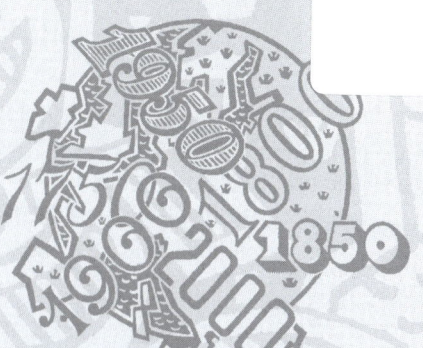

A2 History
UNIT 6

Edexcel

Hitler and the Nazi State: Power and Control, 1933–39

Geoff Stewart

Series Editor: Derrick Murphy

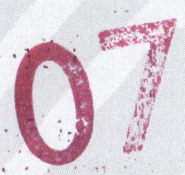

A2 History

Philip Allan Updates
Market Place
Deddington
Oxfordshire
OX15 0SE

tel: 01869 338652
fax: 01869 337590
e-mail: sales@philipallan.co.uk
www.philipallan.co.uk

© Philip Allan Updates 2002

ISBN 0 86003 736 3

All rights reserved; no part of this publication may be reproduced, stored in a retrieval system, or transmitted, in any form or by any means, electronic, mechanical, photocopying, recording or otherwise without either the prior written permission of Philip Allan Updates or a licence permitting restricted copying in the United Kingdom issued by the Copyright Licensing Agency Ltd, 90 Tottenham Court Road, London W1P 9HE.

In all cases we have attempted to trace and credit copyright owners of material used.

This Guide has been written specifically to support students preparing for the Edexcel A2 History Unit 6 examination. The content has been neither approved nor endorsed by Edexcel and remains the sole responsibility of the author.

Printed by Information Press, Eynsham, Oxford

Contents

Introduction

Aims of the unit 4

The examination paper 5

How to use this guide 5

Sources 6

Examinable skills 9

Content Guidance

About this section 12

Outline of topics 13

Introductory survey 14

The political structures of the Third Reich 24

Himmler and terror 27

Goebbels and propaganda 32

Goering and the economy 35

Opposition and resistance 39

Questions and Answers

About this section 44

Question 1 45

Question 2 56

Question 3 65

Question 4 76

Question 5 86

A2 History

Introduction

Aims of the unit

Unit 6 amounts to 20% of the whole A-level course or 40% of the A2 award. It requires both knowledge of the topic and the ability to assess and use the source material provided. The expected source-handling skills will be developed from those required at AS level but, as is appropriate to A2, will be more demanding. The difficulty of source material and the types of question asked will also be more demanding than those for Unit 1 at AS.

Unit 6 has 30 marks. These are split roughly into 12 marks for knowledge of the topic and 18 marks for ability to handle the sources. Handling the sources is defined as:

the ability to interpret, evaluate and use a range of source material and explain and evaluate interpretations of historical events and topics studied.

Knowledge involves the ability to:

recall, select and deploy historical knowledge accurately, and communicate knowledge and understanding of history in a clear and effective manner.

It also involves being able to:

present historical explanations showing understanding of appropriate concepts and arriving at substantiated judgements.

What all this means is that the emphasis of this unit is on the ability to comprehend and manipulate the extracts, rather than on simple knowledge of the Nazi state. Unlike Unit 1, there are only two questions, both of which are tests of skill in comprehension and assessment of the sources, and knowledge. A really good answer is one that blends knowledge and sources, with a sharp focus on the question. All the skills acquired in previous units should come into play in this final synoptic unit of assessment — 'synoptic' because it is meant to draw together the skills learned throughout the course. The skills used in Unit 1 — simple comprehension, awareness of inference, evaluation and comparison of sources — should all be brought into play where appropriate and blended with the essay skills developed for Units 2, 3 and 4.

The first question will involve making and supporting a judgement on the key features of an episode, historical movement or issue. These key features could relate to the strengths and weaknesses of a historical movement, the role and aims of individuals mentioned in the specification, or attitudes towards these historical figures and movements. Candidates will be expected to draw upon their understanding of a range of historical perspectives and make use of their own knowledge linked to three of the source extracts.

The second question will require the candidate to use all the extracts in making and supporting a judgement about historical interpretation. Candidates will be presented with an interpretation and will be invited to make and support a judgement about its truth. The question is likely to start with either 'to what extent' or 'how far do you agree with the opinion...?'

Clearly the second question is more demanding, not least in its requirement that all the sources be used. And it is important to take note of the number of marks allocated to each section and to make sure that your effort is proportionate to the spread of marks. The response to question (b), which is worth 20 marks, should be roughly twice as long as the response to question (a), which can earn only 10 marks.

The aim of this unit is to teach candidates to appreciate how historians construct an argument from a range of primary and secondary sources to support or challenge a historical interpretation. What an undergraduate is expected to do in a week or over many weeks when writing an essay after labouring in the library, is here concentrated into two mini-tasks spread over an hour and three-quarters. The examiner has helped by selecting an appropriate group of sources, but the essential historical skills of comprehension and evaluation followed by the construction and presentation of an argument are all required.

The examination paper

Five examples of questions and answers are given in the last section of this book. The features of an examination paper in this unit will be as follows:
- First the sources will be given. There will be either five or six of these, together adding up to no more than 800 words. At least two of the sources will be secondary sources and at least two will be primary. None of the sources will usually be visual, but they could be statistical.
- Before each source, information on its provenance will be given in italics. This is of the utmost importance in helping you to comprehend it and/or assess its usefulness in helping you to answer the question.
- Much greater emphasis is placed on secondary sources in Unit 6 than in Unit 1. Candidates should take note of the author and date of publication of each secondary source, as this could be a pointer as to which side of the argument in a historical interpretation the extract is supporting. More is said about this on page 6, under the heading 'Sources'.
- After the sources, the two questions appear. The layout of the questions in a typical examination paper will be as follows:

Answer both questions (a) and (b).
(a) Using your own knowledge and the evidence of sources 1, 2 and 3, explain how…
(10 marks)
(b) Using your own knowledge and the evidence of all five sources, how far do you agree that…
(20 marks)

How to use this guide

First, make sure you understand clearly the pattern of marks and the types of question explained above.

Although the emphasis of this unit is on the handling of sources rather than knowledge, there is still a body of facts to be learned. Carefully study the outline of the

content required, which is given in the Content Guidance section. Try to:
- master the vocabulary and the concepts given there
- sort out clearly in your mind the important individuals who figure in the events of these years
- remember the people in terms of the areas of their importance

Perhaps the most important part of the guide is the Question and Answer section, which provides five examples of the kinds of question you will be asked. It is important to work through these, studying the two sets of sample answers provided and the examiner's comments (preceded by the icon ℮). The first example is deliberately designed as an A-grade response which, although not perfect, gives a good idea of what is required. The purpose of the second answer is to illustrate some of the common errors that students make.

Sources

A vast range of secondary sources is available to any student studying Nazi Germany. New books appear almost daily on the subject. According to one count made in 1997, there were 120,000 publications on Adolf Hitler worldwide. The next year Hitler attracted another 700 pages in the form of Volume 1 of Ian Kershaw's magnificent biography *Hitler*, published by Allen Lane. One excellent study by Michael Burleigh, entitled simply *The Third Reich* and published by Macmillan in 2000, points out in the introduction that the topic of one chapter alone has 55,000 relevant publications.

There are many collections of primary documents, and students should familiarise themselves with some of the different types of material available. The Question and Answer section contains an assortment of these. As with all sources of evidence used by historians, it is important to try to find out *why* a particular document was written, and of course *when*. Usually the date will be given in italics before the extract and some information will generally be provided to help you understand why this particular source was originally produced. Clearly it helps to know the political sympathies of the author.

Is he or she a Nazi sympathiser or supporter? Obviously the *Diaries of Joseph Goebbels* need treating with caution in this sense. It is worth knowing that they appear to have been written with publication in mind. The author was a privileged member of Hitler's inner circle and a perceptive observer and writer, but like all historical documents his diaries need treating with some care if they are used as evidence.

Is the author an opponent of the Nazis, such as Victor Klemperer, a Jewish professor and Nazi victim? He wrote detailed diaries covering these years, which were published in English translation in 1998. Memoirs pose special problems, apart from the question of bias. A well-known example is the memoir by an English woman married to an anti-Nazi German, Christabel Bielenberg, published by Corgi in 1970. Her account of life in the Third Reich is entitled *The Past is Myself*, and was written some time after the events it describes. Bias and the influence of hindsight must be acknowledged, but this doesn't mean the source is worthless to historians.

One of the most fascinating books offering insight into the workings of the Third Reich is that written by Albert Speer while he was imprisoned in the 1960s and entitled simply *Inside the Third Reich* (Weidenfield, 1970). Speer was an intelligent insider with access to Hitler, and a regular attender at his dinner parties. He knew all the senior Nazis and during the war became one of Hitler's most powerful ministers. Once again it is a source written with hindsight and with an agenda. Despite this, it remains an invaluable window through which we can peer into the world of the 1930s.

One key element in the specification concerns the state of public opinion and the popularity of the Nazi regime. Given the absence of opinion polls under the Nazi regime, there are real problems for a historian seeking to make an assessment. Two well-known sources are often used. The first is the hundreds of reports to the government from the SD, the SS information service. The authors of these reports were told to be scrupulous in assessing discontent. In consequence, they tend to be fairly pessimistic about the level of support that the regime enjoyed.

The second well-known source of information on public opinion is the 'Reports from Germany', drawn up for the Social Democratic Party in exile. Unlike the reports of the SS, these tend to see conformity everywhere and to downplay the level of discontent. As the French historian Pierre Aycoberry wrote in his book *The Social History of the Third Reich* (The New Press, 1999), 'the police saw potential rebels on every side, while those who resisted the regime detected cowards or accomplices everywhere'.

Of course, people's opinions change over time and with circumstances. Hitler himself and the Nazi Party were no exception. Two of the most important sources of information used by historians in their study of the Nazi Party and regime are *Mein Kampf* ('My Struggle') written by Hitler in 1924 and regularly used to illustrate Hitler's opinions on a variety of subjects, and the so-called *25 Points*, the programme of the Nazi Party written in 1920. How important these two documents are is open to much debate. Some have argued that Hitler was later ashamed and embarrassed by much of what he had written in 1924, and that *Mein Kampf* should be taken with a pinch of salt. Even more doubt has been cast on the value of *25 Points*, written as it was in the very early days of the party. The Nazi Party of 1920 was very different from the mass party of 1933. The relevance of these two documents, dating from the period of the party's struggle and even impotence, in assessing the ruling party of 1933–39 is open to question.

The Nazi Party was particularly adept at adjusting to circumstances. In some ways it was all things to all people because it lacked a clear-cut message. It was both socialist and nationalist, as its name implies. It is not clear even now whether Hitler should be considered a figure of the left or the right. Traditionally he is considered a figure of the right, particularly by Marxists and those of left-wing persuasion. Yet to many conservatives he was a dangerous figure of the left, closely related to the very Communists he denounced. Many of the Nazis' most bitter opponents between 1933 and 1945 came from the ranks of the aristocracy and the traditional right.

One of the big questions within this topic is who benefited from the Nazi regime, and historians have tried for decades to answer it. Many of the extracts used in the

Question and Answer section are concerned with this. The dates of such extracts must always be taken into account. The supporter of 1933 could become the disillusioned opponent of 1938: General Ludwig Beck, chief of the Army General Staff from 1935 to 1938, was the centre of much army opposition to Hitler in 1938. Yet in 1933 he had greeted Hitler's accession to power with the words: 'I have wished for years for the political revolution, and now my wishes have come true. It is the first ray of hope since 1918.'

You must pay attention to the social class of the writer, as this may be of vital importance. There was considerable variation in support from one area of the country to another, and the importance of geography should be noted if such information is provided with the extract. However, the fact that Ludwig Beck, a general from the Rhineland, opposed Hitler does not mean that all generals or all Rhinelanders did the same.

W. S. Allen, an American historian, undertook a pioneering study of a single German town, Northeim near Hanover. He published his findings in a book entitled *The Nazi Seizure of Power* (Eyre and Spottiswood, 1965). It contains a mass of fascinating insights that help to explain the initial Nazi success, and the nature of the Nazi regime as it impacted on one small German community. But it is vital to remember that this one small German town was atypical in the level of support it showed for the Nazi Party in 1933. In the last free elections in March of that year, the Nazis secured two-thirds of the vote in Northeim compared to a nationwide total of two-fifths. This might clearly be relevant when considering the relatively low level of fear and intimidation within the town over the next 6 years.

Statistical data have their own special pitfalls. Always look carefully to see what is being offered — once again, dates are important. When economic data are on offer, make sure you understand what is referred to. For example, is it 'real wages' (i.e. what such wages can buy with given prices) or 'money wages'? It is important not to be intimidated by the appearance of statistical data. There may be lies, damned lies and statistics, but statistics are a very useful way of presenting a complex mass of information simply.

Since the questions asked in this unit are matters of controversy among historians, it is necessary to address the role of **historiography**. History is the study of the past; historiography is the study of the study of the past, i.e. how historians over the years have differed or agreed in their interpretations. The Nazi regime has been subject to the attention of so many historians that historiographical controversies abound. These are referred to in the appropriate parts of the Content Guidance section. There are two outstanding books to underpin this course: one is *Nazism*, edited by Neil Gregor in the Oxford Reader Series, published in 2000. For primary documents and an excellent commentary, see Volume 2 of *Nazism, a Documentary Reader*, edited by J. Noakes and G. Pridham, new edition published by Exeter Univerisity Press in 2000.

You will encounter a welter of debate and controversy, but this does not mean you should become cynical about the pursuit of truth. The fact that history is 'argument without end' is its greatest joy, and the realisation that there is always a counter-argument makes it an important educational discipline. The end product should be tolerance, not cynicism.

If candidates show an awareness of a particular debate among historians and can relate this to the question asked, they will obviously be rewarded. This does not mean you should learn a list of historians and chant their names in your answers. But if the mention of a particular historian strengthens your argument, then it is a good idea to make the point. However, historiographical knowledge is no more valuable than any other sort of knowledge you can use when answering the questions. The most important thing is that the knowledge should be relevant and should advance the argument being made.

Examinable skills

The ability to comprehend a source is perhaps the most basic requirement in this unit. To achieve this there is no substitute for simple practice. Analysis, evaluation and interpretation follow on from the basic capacity for comprehension.

Remember that the comprehension is needed in the context of the questions set. Try to see where a particular source belongs in terms of the argument you are going to make. Does it support, or contradict, an opinion? For example, if you are pursuing an argument about whether Hitler was a strong or weak dictator, does a particular source show him to be rigidly in control, or completely relaxed about delegating power to others? It might be useful to go through the sources indicating support or contradiction with + or –, perhaps in different colours for the two questions. Always remember that a particular extract might offer both support and contradiction.

Try to interlink different sources, pointing out where one source supports or contradicts another with regard to a particular detail. It is essential to select the appropriate passage to do this well. The selections quoted should be as brief as possible, and it is important to avoid simply paraphrasing the sources.

You should try to develop the skill of making the appropriate inference and deduction from extracts. A source might appear at one level to be making a supporting point but might conceal an implication which can be used in the opposing argument. Always take into account the provenance of the extract. The key information about this is deliberately provided to give you a steer and a clue. It may affect the reliance you can place upon the extract, or it may contain valuable information in its own right.

Don't leave it until the final sentence before you openly address the question. Try always to make a clear opening statement that indicates the direction your answer is taking, and if possible include a reference to the sources in your opening paragraph. Develop your points in a logical and structured way with appropriate quotations and support from the extracts. No paragraph should be without reference to a source, and the ideal one will interweave more than one source with your own knowledge. Try to avoid using the sources in the order in which they appear on the paper — you should be using the extracts, not allowing yourself to be dictated to by them.

Avoid the use of prepared answers about bias and the nature of primary and secondary sources. It must be emphasised that your evaluation of a source will be for a specific purpose. Your answer must constantly show awareness of the specific points in the question.

One of the skills examined is the ability to:

communicate clear, concise and logical arguments substantiated by relevant evidence.

The ability to write clearly and attractively is one of the most valuable in the historian's armoury. It is a skill to be worked on constantly. There is no quick way to achieve literary polish, but as in all essays there should be a clear introductory statement and, most important of all, a conclusion to draw together the argument advanced throughout the answer. In the conclusion, as in the introduction, reference should be made to at least one source.

Content Guidance

The specification for this option of Unit 6 is divided into two major bullet points, each with two subordinate points that summarise content requirements. These are as follows:

- How popular was Nazi rule in Germany 1933–39?
  — the legacy of the Weimar government in explaining initial support for the Nazi regime: acceptance of, and support for, Nazi rule among different social, economic and religious groups
  — Nazi propaganda and the use of terror: the nature and extent of resistance to Nazi rule
- Hitler: 'weak dictator' or 'master in the Third Reich'?
  — structure of the Nazi state and personal role of Hitler
  — power of Hitler's lieutenants: Goebbels, Goering and Himmler

The main focus is upon the growth and development of the Nazi regime between March 1933 and September 1939, and reactions to it. It will be necessary to understand why Hitler and the Nazis so detested the Weimar Republic and how influential the experiences of 1929–33 were in shaping the policies and structures of the Third Reich and the popular responses to these. No questions on foreign policy as such will be set, but a knowledge of its impact on the regime is clearly desirable. To help you appreciate what is required, the subject matter of Unit 6 has been broken down in the Content Guidance section in two ways. First, there is an outline of topics, for use as a checklist for revision before the exam. The six sections that follow give more detail on the concepts, personalities and basic data required in the specification. Where appropriate, each subsection is followed by listings of concepts and key figures. Words that appear in these listings are emboldened in the text.

Edexcel Unit 6

Outline of topics

Introductory survey
Weimar Germany and its legacy for the Third Reich
Nazi ideology — left or right?
The consolidation of power, March 1933–August 1934
The authoritarian regime, 1934–37
Radicalisation, 1938–39

The political structures of the Third Reich
Hitler's role and position
The dual state and competing empires

Himmler and terror
Heinrich Himmler and the SS
The Gestapo and the SD
The *Kripo*
Concentration camps
Assessment of the role of terror

Goebbels and propaganda
Josef Goebbels
The press
Radio
Film
Ritual and rallies

Goering and the economy
Hermann Goering
The four-year plan, 1936–37
The Blomberg–Fritsch Affair, 1938
Living standards — winners and losers

Opposition and resistance
The workers and the political left
The role of the churches
The army
Resistenz (non-conformity)
Assessment

Introductory survey

Weimar Germany and its legacy for the Third Reich

The **Second Reich** died suddenly and unexpectedly at 2 p.m. on 9 November 1918. Philipp Scheidemann, the second most important socialist MP, ended a speech to a cheering crowd in Berlin with the words: 'Long live the Republic!' He seems to have been carried away by the excitement of the moment. His words did not please Friedrich Ebert, the leader of the party. They certainly did not please a temporarily blinded German corporal lying in hospital. Adolf Hitler, in *Mein Kampf*, later recalled how he heard the news of the downfall of the monarchy with horror. This was intensified when, with his sight restored, he returned to Munich and saw at first hand the Red Bavarian Republic under Kurt Eisner, a Jewish Marxist. It was probably at this moment that a jumble of prejudices against Jews, Marxists and enemies of Germany crystallised into a quasi-religious mission.

Germany had in 1914 been the greatest power in Europe. It had the world's most powerful army and the world's second most powerful navy. In every way Germany appeared to be one of the world's leading nations. By 1919 this navy was rusting at the bottom of Scapa Flow, and the German army had been reduced to a paltry 100,000. Territory had been lost to Germany's neighbours; at home half a million Germans had died of starvation brought about by the British blockade; and inflation was gathering pace. By 1923 inflation had turned to hyperinflation and conveniently wiped out the debts of the government, at the expense of ruining many members of the middle classes who had lent money to the government during the war. Thus right from the start the Weimar Republic was associated in many Germans' minds with defeat, national humiliation and misery.

The memories of 1918–19 were vital in shaping many of the key features of the Third Reich. Hitler, like many in the army, was obsessed with the idea of 'the stab in the back', the notion that Germany had not really been defeated by enemy armies but by traitors at home, notably Jews and Marxists who had organised strikes and revolution. He was determined that this would never happen again. The next time Germany went to war — and he certainly intended that it should go to war again — there would be no internal enemies to weaken the Reich.

The Weimar Republic had looked destined to fail in its early years, beset by opponents of the extreme right and extreme left. Yet by the mid-1920s it did appear to have a future. Economic prosperity returned, and with it some degree of political stability. The aged Field Marshal Paul von Hindenburg had agreed to stand as president in 1925 and this *ersatz* (substitute) Kaiser, as he has been termed, gave a certain degree of respectability to the young republic. Gustav Stresemann, as foreign minister from 1924 to 1929, improved Germany's international standing and began successfully to moderate the harsh conditions of the Treaty of Versailles. The real wages of most workers rose. The republic had conferred enhanced trade union rights together with an extension of welfare benefits. Most of the states and cities extended community facilities for the masses. Germany, like America, was entering the world of mass consumption and prosperity. This period was not one of success for Adolf Hitler. There seemed little future for a cult leader offering salvation and redemption to a people who saw little need to be saved.

Yet all was not well. 'We are dancing on the volcano', pronounced Stresemann. Certain segments of Weimar society were not sharing in the prosperity. The most notable group to miss out were the farmers, who amounted to a third of Germany's population. Farm prices were depressed, with the world awash with cheap food. Prices fell steeply from 1927, bringing misery to many rural areas. It is no accident that it was among these suffering agricultural regions that the Nazis made their first great electoral breakthroughs.

Much of Weimar's prosperity was based on borrowing. The federal government in Berlin borrowed rather than face difficult decisions about raising taxes or cutting spending. Locally, the **Länder** and cities borrowed to finance welfare and community projects. There was a tide of money crossing the Atlantic to fund the new democratic Germany. Once this flow of money ceased in 1929 — and it was already drying up in 1928 — really difficult decisions faced the politicians of Germany. And given the political system of the Weimar Republic, difficult decisions were well-nigh impossible to take. The Reichstag was elected by proportional representation, which produced a multitude of parties mostly organised along class lines. Only the Catholic Centre Party transcended class — it spoke for the large Roman Catholic religious minority of the south and west. The bitter class and religious divisions of German society could be fudged and forgotten during a period of prosperity, although every government had to be a coalition as no one party achieved a majority. The biggest and most important party was the Social Democratic Party of Germany (SPD), with approximately a quarter of the vote, but it competed for working-class favour with the Communist Party of Germany (KPD). These Moscow-directed Communists were bitter enemies of the more moderate SPD. Several parties competed for the middle-class vote.

This system broke down in March 1930, when no government could be organised that commanded a majority in the Reichstag. The SPD wanted tax increases and the middle-class parties wanted cuts in spending as the slump deepened. From this date, government could function only by ruling through presidential decree. The jobless total climbed alarmingly, and with it the misery index of German society. By 1932, 5.9 million people were officially unemployed, but in reality probably far more were without work. The rural population were nominally employed but were living on pittances, with bankrupt farms facing takeover from the banks. Small shopkeepers' incomes nose-dived as consumption fell.

Suicides in the Germany of 1932 were four times the rate in Britain. Crime escalated. In 1927 there had been 48,477 cases of armed robbery reported in the state of Prussia. By 1932 it was 99,045. Reported thefts nearly doubled in the same period. Beggars seemed to swarm the streets and newspapers were filled with tales of social collapse featuring drugs, prostitution and every kind of vice. It was easy to argue that Weimar had failed its citizens. Now they would listen to the voice of a messiah.

No longer a voice crying in the wilderness, Hitler piled up votes by the million. Following the elections of July 1932, his National Socialist German Workers' Party (NSDAP or Nazi Party) was overwhelmingly the largest party. It was now impossible to think of forming a parliamentary government that did not include the Nazis. They had built up a broad basis of support that transcended class and religious lines, a unique feat for Weimar Germany. They appealed to some of those who rejected the new republic and dreamed of returning to 1914 with all its certainties.

The new freedoms of Weimar Germany frightened many outside the big cities. The cultural creativity of the artistic élite, which in Berlin was exciting, seemed to some Germans depravity. Yet it would be wrong to think of the Nazis as a party intent on putting the clock back — it was in essence a young person's party. It was to youth that it spoke when it promised a brave new world. Hitler was 43 when he became Chancellor, and he contrasted with the much older politicians who had dominated the republic hitherto. Goebbels was 35 in 1933 and Himmler only 33. The party appealed to idealism with the dream of a united, classless, reinvigorated Germany, dynamic yet orderly. As one young worker put it in explaining why he joined the party: 'The joy of fighting for Hitler's principle gave my life a new meaning. The philosophy of the movement endowed my hitherto aimless life with a meaning and purpose.'

The language of redemption and religious transformation is even more obvious in the case of this young professional: 'When I joined the party, my life once again came to have significance. I had to neglect my family to some extent; nevertheless I was satisfied. My very family had to admit I was a changed man.'

Hitler and the party offered simple truths that could be easily digested, and promised a new beginning. All that was required was faith in the leader. Catchy phrases and 'spin' were to continue to substitute for real political debate throughout the Third Reich, drawing attention to the miseries of Weimar and contrasting it with the new Nazi paradise of, for instance, law and order: 'Then [pre-1933]: no punishment without law. Now: no crime without punishment.'

Following their triumph in the elections of July 1932, the Nazis had to wait until January 1933 for Hitler to receive the Chancellorship from President Hindenburg. The old Field Marshal was deeply reluctant to accept him as Chancellor. But the rise in support for the Communist Party convinced many of the old élite that the only way of avoiding revolution or civil war was to appoint Hitler. In the words of one eminent historian, he was levered into power, but this was only because he commanded more popular support than any other German politician. Conservative and **monarchist** politicians like Franz von Papen and Alfred Hugenberg, leader of the Germany National People's Party (DNVP), were convinced that they could control and use this populist messiah to transform the republic and possibly restore the monarchy.

In one sense his appointment was a return to democracy. It was hoped to produce a government with a majority in the Reichstag for the first time since March 1930, and thereby end the need to rule by presidential decree. The cabinet of which Hitler was the nominal head was filled with conservatives, not Nazis.

Two months later it was clear that Hitler had out-manoeuvred his conservative allies. The Enabling Bill conferred upon the Chancellor and his cabinet the legislative powers of the Reichstag. Hermann Goering, as one of only three Nazi ministers, had supplemented the police with 50,000 SA (*Sturmabteilung*) auxiliaries, and under the Emergency Decree of 28 February, thousands of people were arrested. On 22 March Heinrich Himmler, the new police chief in Munich, opened Dachau as a 'rehabilitation' centre for enemies of the Reich. The new age had begun.

Nazi ideology — left or right?

The twin ideas at the basis of Hitler's political life, racialism and nationalism, seem to have been absorbed before the First World War. However, it was the events of 1918 and 1919 that translated prejudices and **anti-Semitism** into passions. Hitler blamed the defeat of Germany in 1918 on the Jews, and in Munich where he returned in 1919, Jews played a large part in the aborted revolution. Hitler created in his mind a vast, all-embracing Jewish conspiracy to 'destroy civilisation'. Were not Jews dominant among the Bolsheviks in Russia? Was it not Jewish capital in America, Britain and France that had mobilised those countries for the defeat of Germany? Passion and hatred gave power to his voice. The simplicity of his message ensured a favourable reception in the right circumstances.

He offered a new political religion, shaped for the age of the common man. Even before the First World War all those devices that would have kept Hitler firmly in check were weakening. The German philosopher Nietzsche had famously declared that God was dead. Traditional religion was losing its grip. The old ruling élites were being challenged. An age of mass consumption and mass ideas was being born. In place of kings and emperors, politicians told the people what they wanted to hear in language they could readily grasp. The First World War speeded the destruction of the old world, particularly in Germany. With the Kaiser gone, a new icon was needed. The returning disillusioned troops were particularly vulnerable to the sort of simplistic message that Hitler propounded. The war had brutalised many and made violence respectable. The new NSDAP, founded in 1920, was to provide a home for soldiers like Ernst Röhm, who flaunted his contempt for conventional morality. The displaced Baltic German Alfred Rosenberg, fleeing from the Bolsheviks, also joined the new party, echoing Hitler's bitter anti-Jewish sentiments and racial analysis of the world. Rosenberg made his biggest contribution to National Socialist ideology in his book *The Myth of the Twentieth Century*, published in 1930. Goebbels described it as 'a great intellectual belch', but it was generally considered second only to *Mein Kampf* in the canon of writings that expounded National Socialism.

It was once fashionable to see National Socialism not as an ideology but as a cover for the pursuit of power. One of the first English biographers of Hitler, Alan Bullock, takes this line, in *Hitler*, Penguin 1962:

> *The sole theme of the Nazi revolution was domination, dressed up in the doctrine of race, and failing that, a vindictive destructiveness.*

This is to underestimate the coherence and the consistency of Hitler's faith. He was an utterly sincere believer, and this sincerity gave power to his message. The German historian Eberhard Jaeckel demonstrated this in his *Hitler's* **Weltanschauung**, published in 1969 and revised in 1991. Bullock himself came to accept it and recognises the importance of ideology in his *Hitler and Stalin*, published in 1991.

National Socialism as expounded by Hitler and Rosenberg was woven from many intellectual strands. Its origins lay with those thinkers who had rejected the **enlightenment** of the eighteenth century, with its emphasis on reason and the essential goodness and rationality of man — the spirit of the French Revolution. Goebbels was to proclaim in 1933: 'we have abolished 1789'. Instead of liberty and reason, there was an emphasis on obedience and faith. Instead of fulfilment through thought, there was fulfilment through action, preferably violent action. Men were essentially killers, not philosophers, and women were the instruments for producing more killers. The pram was the woman's tank. The Nazis saw the enlightenment and its ideology, liberalism, as wholly destructive of the warrior mentality.

One of the earliest and greatest of enlightenment thinkers, Spinoza, had been Jewish. The enlightenment had brought with it toleration of Jews. It had also spawned capitalism and democracy, both also viewed with suspicion by the Nazis. Hitler denounced democracy in *Mein Kampf* as destructive of the principle of leadership (*Führerprinzip*):

> *Does anybody honestly believe that human progress originates in the composite brain of the majority and not in the brain of the individual personality?*

There was a denunciation of what were seen as the misplaced humanitarian values of the enlightenment. Like one of the first and most savage critics of the French Revolution, Joseph de Maistre, who had called for brutal punishment as the only solution to human weakness and the only alternative to anarchy, the Nazi regime emphasised punishment as the solution to the social crisis of Weimar.

Karl Marx had seen the dynamic of history as class conflict. To the Nazis, it was conflict between races. Racial conflict was the engine of progress, and the Jew was the eternal enemy of the Germanic race whether in the guise of an American capitalist or a Russian Bolshevik. The concept of class conflict, developed into an all-embracing theory by the Jewish Marx, was seen as another trick to keep the Germanic race weak and divided.

The Nazis claimed to offer a third way, between capitalism and communism, and at the heart of this was the concept of the community, *Gemeinschaft*. It was this that had considerable appeal for many Germans both before 1933 and afterwards. As one rail worker wrote, 'National Socialism, with its promise of a community of blood, a barring of all class struggle, attracted me profoundly'. Throughout the Third Reich it was a concept that was prominently promoted, but it was a *Volksgemeinschaft*, a racial community, excluding the racial enemies.

Many commentators have placed National Socialism on the extreme right of the political spectrum. It espoused much that was conservative, particularly in the visual arts. Marxist writers and historians have traditionally seen it as the last attempt of a dying capitalism to defend itself. Walter Ulbricht, German Communist exile and later head of the East German state, declared the Nazi regime to be 'the terroristic dictatorship of the most reactionary, chauvinistic, and imperialist elements of German finance capital'. With these views in mind, the Soviet Union and the international Communist community initially welcomed the coming to power of the Nazis as the inevitable first stage of the downfall of German capitalism. They were clearly wrong. On the other side of the political spectrum, devout conservatives saw National Socialism as a revolutionary creed akin to **Marxism**, but a brown plague instead of a red one. Ewald von Kleist-Schmenzin, a conservative nationalist, wrote in 1932 that the Nazis' 'domestic programme is synonymous with Social Democracy on economic, social and tax policy'. It was after all a socialist creed, constantly stressing the common good. Men like Goebbels appear to have been genuinely radical and even revolutionary in the transformation they wished to see in German society.

It was in fact on both the left and the right, as the name National Socialist implies. Its central characteristic, which it shared with Marxism, was a sweeping belief system. It offered certainties in an uncertain world. It claimed to provide answers. Goebbels, Himmler, Rosenberg and above all Hitler were all believers, and all the more effective as salesmen for believing in what they peddled. The Nazi Party also attracted a chilling group of technocrats who were not believers in the same sense — Goering, Albert Speer and above all Reinhard Heydrich were attracted by the emphasis on action regardless of moral consequence. This combination of fanatics and ruthless managers was likely either to produce a brave new world, or to conjure up hell.

The consolidation of power, March 1933–August 1934

In August 1934, Hitler added the title of President to that of Chancellor, following the death of President Hindenburg. He tended not to use the title, preferring the simpler one of Führer. But he was like an absolute monarch, wielding power akin to that of Frederick the Great in the eighteenth century. Now no one could dismiss him — only assassination or an army coup could remove him. In the event, it would take the combined armies of the three most powerful nations in the world and his own suicide to achieve this.

Over 17 months before August 1934, the ground was being prepared for this final act of consolidation. In spring 1933 the civil service was purged of opponents. The vast majority of employees remained in post, but hastened to join the NSDAP. Powers were taken to bring the governments of the Länder into line. Their formal independence was not abolished until January 1934, when Germany at last became a unitary state. On 2 May 1933, the trade unions were abolished and replaced by the German Labour Front (**DAF**) under the Nazi Robert Ley. The workers were given 1 May as an annual holiday, a long-standing objective of the unions. In June and July all other political parties were either abolished, as in the case of the SPD, or went into voluntary liquidation like the DNVP. Germany was now a one-party state. More Nazis were appointed to cabinet posts, such as Josef Goebbels, and troublesome conservatives like Hugenberg of the DNVP were persuaded to retire.

These crucial high-profile changes in Berlin were matched at local level by local Nazi bosses. Germany was coordinated down to the most trivial level. Choirs and chess clubs as well as town halls surrendered themselves to new Nazi masters. In Northeim, the Social Democrat Choir was disbanded and the more respectable middle-class one was Nazified. The town's shooting club invited Ernst Girmann, the Nazi leader in the town, to become its captain. The town's library was purged of any books that caused offence to the new masters.

Initially, this whole process was carried out against a background of chaotic SA violence and intimidation. Illegal camps sprang up to hold alleged opponents of the regime. The whole process is colourfully described by Rudolf Diels, the first head of the Prussian political police. He was a conservative, not a Nazi, and was eventually pushed out by Himmler in 1934. His memoirs, published in 1949, are a useful source for these early days of the Third Reich, but like all memoirs they need to be treated with caution. Diels describes the release of tortured and beaten prisoners from makeshift SA prisons. When he was thanked by Hitler for his work against the Communists, he allegedly told the new head of Germany that his biggest problem was the SA, not the Communists.

Clearly the SA *had* become a problem. In August 1933, Goering sought to restore discipline within the police by removing the 50,000 auxiliaries who had been enrolled earlier in the year. They had done their work and played a notable part in making possible the tightening Nazi grip on power. However, Hitler did not want to frighten his middle-class supporters or too many of his conservative allies. Attacks on foreigners were becoming too common and it was now necessary to achieve stability and respectability. The SA, however, expected to inherit power in all its forms and not to see bourgeois civil servants like Diels continue in their jobs. Too few of the SA chiefs had been rewarded for the discontent to be assuaged, and this discontent was to build up to a bloody climax in June 1934, with the Night of the Long Knives.

By early 1934 Hitler was facing a double problem. The old Field Marshal was clearly not going to live much longer and Hitler wished to succeed him. For this, the support of the army was necessary and the army chiefs, notably General von Blomberg, the Minister of War, were deeply worried by Röhm's ambition to become Minister of War and integrate the army into the SA. Some other Nazi chieftains, notably Goering and Himmler, were also worried by Röhm's power and ambition. His homosexual orgies were also beginning to become an embarrassment to the new regime. On the other side of the political spectrum there was a growing threat from the conservative right, who were frightened by Nazi excesses and hoped that with the death of Hindenburg the monarchy could be restored. Plots began to develop to this end around Edgar Jung, a young friend of the vice-chancellor von Papen.

The answer to these twin problems was a hail of bullets on the last day of June 1934. Goering and Himmler appear to have done the detailed planning. It is sometimes suggested that they fabricated evidence of a plot to convince a reluctant Hitler to sanction Röhm's murder. Whatever the true origins of the bloody events of 30 June, they enhanced Hitler's power and he easily succeeded to the presidency a month later. The army had supplied weapons for the bloodbath, and now that the SA were cut down to size they were happy to swear an oath of allegiance to the new Führer.

To most respectable middle-class Germans, these events were seen as a cruel necessity. Germany could now return to law and order. The murder of a few respectable conservatives like Edgar Jung amongst the carnage wrought on the SA was conveniently forgotten.

The transformation of the republic into a one-party dictatorship within the space of 18 months was a remarkable achievement. It was made possible by a combination of circumstances. First, it was done gradually — the salami approach, slice by slice. For most Germans it appeared to be a legal process. More often than not, the formalities of law were respected or, as was the case with the Night of the Long Knives, it could be portrayed as a return to law and order through unpleasant but necessary measures.

The weakness and divisions of the Nazis' opponents made resistance difficult. The trade unions were weakened by the slump. The parties of the left were bitterly divided. The Communists hated the SPD almost more than the Nazis. The middle class took the SPD at its word, believing its Marxist rhetoric and seeing it as little better than the Communists. The Catholic Church was terrified of Marxism and saw Hitler as the lesser of two evils. Finally, the economic and social crisis of 1929–33 made ordinary Germans turn to extraordinary politicians. It should not be forgotten that the Nazis were a mass party — it was not a few conniving politicians in Berlin bringing about change, but a host of enthusiastic young men throughout the country anxious to bring into reality the messianic vision expounded by their cult leader.

The authoritarian regime, 1934–37

In many ways it is easy to see why both Germans and foreigners felt that Nazi Germany was settling down into a conservative if authoritarian state after 1934, somewhat akin to Germany before 1914. With the murder of Röhm and many of his SA chieftains, the wilder spirits of the Nazi movement seemed to have been checked, and stability and respectability had returned to Germany. It is important to remember that Hitler continued to be surrounded by conservative politicians who looked reassuringly familiar. The professional banker Hjalmar Schacht became Minister of Economics and President of the Reichbank. The army under General von Blomberg was allowed to govern itself without Nazi interference. In Northeim the former leader of the local SPD was able to find safe employment in the new army barracks outside the town. The Foreign Office remained under Baron von Neurath, appointed before Hitler came to power. The number of inmates in the camps declined.

The worst aspects of the slump appeared to be over, and as unemployment fell so did street crime. A new prosperity came to Germany. Even the passing of the Nuremberg laws in 1935 could be seen as a moderate regularisation of the position of Jews in Germany. 'Quarter' Jews and 'half' Jews were excluded from the definition of Jewishness, against the wishes of the wilder anti-Semites inside the Nazi Party. Fanatics like Martin Bormann who wished to push a campaign against the churches were held in check. Even anti-Jewish slogans were removed in 1936 at the time of the Olympic Games, and this event seemed to symbolise Germany's return to both international prestige and normality.

Yet this impression was misleading. Himmler continued to expand his police empire and Goebbels maintained a barrage of propaganda. Hitler's priority was rearmament and this eventually brought conflict with the Ministry of Economics, leading to Schacht's resignation in 1937. There were food shortages and a real economic crisis developed in 1935–36, brought about by the pressure of rearmament. There were widespread reports of discontent and by 1937 the numbers detained in the camps were beginning to increase.

Radicalisation, 1938–39

In February 1938 there were a series of important changes in positions of power. The Minister of War resigned following an embarrassing marriage (see page 37) and the Commander in Chief of the army was also induced to resign. The Foreign Minister was replaced by a devoted Nazi, Joachim von Ribbentrop. Hitler himself became Minister of War. The Economics Ministry was given to a Nazi, Walter Funk, and Schacht finally lost all influence when he was dismissed as President of the Reichbank in January 1939.

The Nazis' grip on power had tightened even more. The number of those arrested increased, and attacks on the Jews were stepped up, notably in November 1938 when Goebbels arranged Reich *Kristallnacht*. A much more risky and adventurous foreign policy, which conservatives feared would lead to war, now seemed to be on the agenda. Some senior figures in the army began to contemplate a coup. It was as if the regime had cast off its conservative disguise and now revealed itself as something much more radical and sinister.

Explanations for this change have been hotly debated by historians. **Intentionalists** like Klaus Hildebrand would see it in terms of Hitler's will. This is certainly the explanation advanced by Albert Speer in his memoirs, drawing attention as he does to Hitler's increasing concern with his health and therefore his need to take action while he could still do so. Others, of the **functionalist** school of historians, seek to explain the changes either in terms of an economic crisis (as does Tim Mason) or, like the eminent German historian Hans Mommsen, as a result of what he termed in 1976 the cumulative radicalisation of Nazi Germany — the inevitable consequence of the chaotic structure of the regime. One of the most chilling aspects of this new extremism was its assault upon the disabled. It began in 1939. There was no new law or official decree, but a few lines typed on Hitler's headed notepaper legitimised the murder of 70,000 mentally handicapped Germans. The moral and legal barriers to any action had now been removed.

Glossary and concepts

anti-Semitism — hostility towards Jews. The word seems to have been coined in 1879, but hostility to Jews goes back centuries before this. There was widespread anti-Jewish feeling in France and Russia in the 1890s. From Russia came one of the most famous pieces of anti-Jewish propaganda, the Protocols of the Elders of Zion. This claimed to show that there was a worldwide Jewish conspiracy, and it certainly influenced many Nazi writers and thinkers.

DAF — German Labour Front under Dr Robert Ley.

enlightenment — the term usually used to describe the dominant intellectual current of the eighteenth century, with its faith in the power of human freedom, science and reason to produce progress. Its roots lay in developments in Holland and Britain in the seventeenth century, when it might be said that liberalism was born.

functionalists/structuralists — historians who reject a Hitler-centred interpretation of the development of the Third Reich and look to its political structures to provide explanations.

Gleichschaltung — policy of 'coordination', whereby the Nazi Party assumed the dominant position in all walks of life. — see pages 19–21.

intentionalists — historians who see Hitler and his views as the driving force in the development of the Third Reich.

Länder — different states of Germany: Prussia (the biggest), Bavaria (second biggest), Saxony, etc. These had been independent until 1871, and until 1933 retained considerable powers of local government.

Marxism — a set of political beliefs based on the works of Karl Marx. Marx claimed to have invented scientific socialism, showing the inevitable triumph of the working class or proletariat over the bourgeoisie. The German Social Democrats claimed to be Marxist, but by 1914 had lost much of their revolutionary fervour. The Bolshevik Revolution in Russia brought revolutionary Marxists to power there and they claimed that they would spread Marxism throughout Europe. Marxists believed in the common ownership of the means of production, distribution and exchange, i.e. they wanted the state to take over most forms of property. This created fear among property-owners.

monarchists — people in Weimar Germany who supported the return of the monarchy and the abolition of the republic. The DNVP was a monarchist party opposed to the revolution of 1918.

Second Reich — name given to the period of German history between 1871 and 1918. The First Reich had ended in 1806 and had dated back to its founder, Charlemagne.

Weltanschauung — world outlook — basic belief system.

The political structures of the Third Reich

Hitler's role and position

'I often asked myself, did Hitler really work?' Albert Speer recorded. He admitted to being baffled by the way Hitler chose to squander his working time. He got up late, often not until lunchtime, went for walks and in the evening watched innumerable films. It was not the lifestyle of a hands-on dictator. One of his aides testified after the war:

> He disliked the study of documents. I have sometimes secured decisions from him, even ones about important matters, without him ever asking to see the relevant files. He took the view that things sorted themselves out, if one did not interfere.

While Hindenburg was alive, Hitler played the part of a conventional Chancellor, sitting at his desk and holding cabinet meetings. Once he became Führer he slipped back into his old disordered habits. The number of cabinet meetings declined steadily from 72 in 1933, to 12 in 1935 and seven in 1937, and finally the last one was held on 5 February 1938. It must be remembered that he was an outsider with limited knowledge of Germany's political system. He had no training or experience to fit him for the job of governing the most powerful nation in Europe. In contrast to most of his political contemporaries, he had not grown up on the inside of politics — as all British prime ministers had done. Stalin in Russia was a party bureaucrat who gained power from inside the Bolshevik Party, thoroughly understanding the twists and bureaucratic turns necessary to govern Soviet Russia.

It is little wonder that the conservative politicians who levered Hitler into power felt that they could use him. It is this lack of active direction or detailed policy that has led some historians to refer to Hitler as a 'weak dictator' and to draw attention to the myriad other centres of power, characterising Nazi Germany as a **polycracy**. Structuralist historians like Hans Mommsen and Martin Broszat have stressed that, to understand the dynamics of Nazi Germany, its complex power structure must be fully appreciated, and it is not enough to explain everything in terms of Hitler's will and intent. Broszat's book *The Hitler State*, published by Longman in 1969, has been particularly influential.

Albert Speer, however, makes sense of this apparent paradox of the dictator who was too lazy to dictate. He refers to Hitler's lifestyle as a product of his artistic temperament:

> He often allowed a problem to mature during the weeks when he seemed entirely taken up with trivial matters. Then, after the 'sudden insight' came, he would spend a few days of intensive work giving final shape to his solution.

The intentionalist school of historians stresses Hitler's role in shaping the Third Reich. Eberhard Jaeckel has attacked the whole notion of polycracy, claiming that the Third Reich was never anything other than a 'monocracy' with Hitler as the sole ruler. These sentiments are echoed by other German historians like Klaus Hildebrande. Some have argued that Hitler deliberately pursued a policy of divide and rule to ensure his supreme authority, and the apparent polycracy of multiple centres of power was an illusion concealing and facilitating Hitler's untrammelled authority. Hans Adolf Jacobsen, in an essay written in 1978 on the structure of National Socialist foreign policy published in *The Third Reich*, C. Leitz (ed.), Blackwell, 1999, admits the confusing multiplicity of structures and the complex decision-making processes, but maintains:

> *Hitler often consciously failed to take clear-cut decisions in order to play individuals off against each other to strengthen his position as the person holding the most important reins and to maintain his absolute position of power.*

Throughout most of the 1970s and 1980s, intentionalist historians threw weighty articles at structuralist historians, and structuralist historians threw even weightier articles back. The whole debate is well covered in Chapter 4 of *The Nazi Dictatorship: Problems and Perspectives of Interpretation*, Arnold, 1993, by Ian Kershaw. Kershaw himself has come close to creating a new consensus around the concept of 'working towards the Führer'. This was clearly expressed in an essay of 1993 and reprinted in Leitz's *The Third Reich*.

Kershaw expresses the same views in his vast, magnificent two-volume biography of Hitler published in 1998 and 2000. He in effect attempts to reconcile the intentionalist and structuralist positions. He accepts the multiplicity of authorities and the chaos of the structure of the Third Reich, but also the power and influence of Hitler in setting the agenda in a vague and generalised way. Other Nazis found a way of clothing Hitler's ideas in detailed policy. Kershaw draws attention to a speech of a Nazi functionary in 1934:

> *Everyone who has the opportunity to observe it knows that the Führer can hardly dictate from above everything which he intends to realise sooner or later. On the contrary, up till now everyone with a post in the new Germany has worked best when he has, so to speak, worked towards the Führer.*

The dual state and competing empires

Almost all historians agree that the political structure of the Nazi state was unusual. As early as 1941 the exiled German Ernst Fraenkel coined the phrase 'the dual state'. There was a Nazi state embodied in institutions like the SS (*Schutzstaffel* – Hitler's élite force) and the DAF, and there was the traditional state embodied in institutions like the army and civil service.

Tension had always existed between them. Nazi radicals had in 1933 hoped to produce a real revolution and transform the traditional German state. But Hitler needed the skills of the civil servants, policemen and army officers, and no amount of enthusiasm from Nazi fanatics could substitute for their professional competence. The result appeared to be a victory for the traditional institutions in 1934. The tension, however, remained — the party was not put to sleep. Under Rudolf Hess and his deputy Martin Bormann it developed into one of many powerful institutions in the Reich. The dualism of state and party was well illustrated by the faction fights surrounding Hitler in the Chancellery.

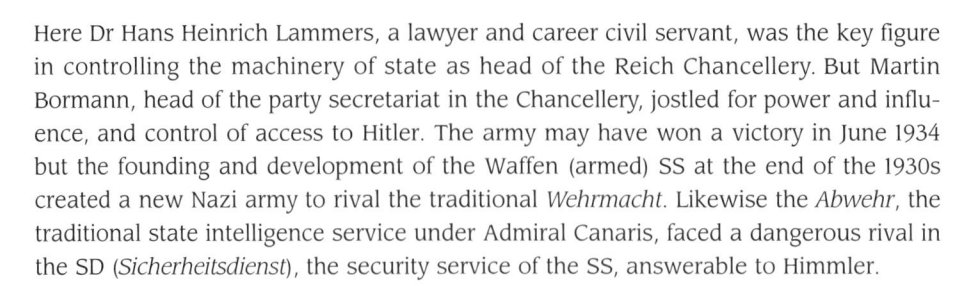

Here Dr Hans Heinrich Lammers, a lawyer and career civil servant, was the key figure in controlling the machinery of state as head of the Reich Chancellery. But Martin Bormann, head of the party secretariat in the Chancellery, jostled for power and influence, and control of access to Hitler. The army may have won a victory in June 1934 but the founding and development of the Waffen (armed) SS at the end of the 1930s created a new Nazi army to rival the traditional *Wehrmacht*. Likewise the *Abwehr*, the traditional state intelligence service under Admiral Canaris, faced a dangerous rival in the SD (*Sicherheitsdienst*), the security service of the SS, answerable to Himmler.

Even within the party there were bitter divisions and competition. The Political Organisation under Dr Robert Ley fought a vicious turf war with the Political Central Commission under Hess and Bormann. Both in their turn struggled with powerful regional Nazi bosses, the **Gauleiter**, who had direct access to Hitler and often behaved like independent medieval barons. This similarity led one historian in 1960, Robert Koehl, to produce an essay entitled 'Feudal aspects of National Socialism' which appeared in the *American Political Science Review*, 54. He writes:

> *One of the most amazing similarities to the feudal system in Nazi administration is the nominal subordinate who acquired power to give his superior orders through appointment by a still higher superior as his personal agent.*

With the takeover of power, the rivalries and traditions of a party based on a personal connection were transferred to the state machine. The result was increasing chaos. This was made worse by a tendency to set up new special institutions and bodies to deal with specific problems. These bodies often became redundant but were never abolished. It is this that led Martin Broszat to write in *The Hitler State* of:

> *the growing decline of the regime's centralised character and its progressive splintering into new centres of activity that tended to devour neighbouring authorities and make themselves indispensable according to the law of motion underlining the leadership principle, increasingly disrupting any rational organisation of government.*

The Third Reich became a hotch-potch of traditional institutions warring with newly created authorities, some claiming to speak for the party and some for the state, and all tracing their authority to the Führer. It was an environment that favoured hard men with sharp elbows. Loyalty to the Führer was essential, but the ability to devour a rival and gobble up his empire before he could do the same to you was an essential prerequisite of survival. Goering, Goebbels and Himmler were all past-masters at this game.

Glossary and concepts

Gauleiter — local/regional Nazi bosses who had often won their areas for the party and as such enjoyed Hitler's thanks and loyalty. Most had direct access to him, giving them real clout. Most were appointed heads of the different states as Rechsstatthalter or state governors after 1933.

Polycracy — term coined to describe a political system where there were many centres of power.

Himmler and terror

Heinrich Himmler and the SS

Heinrich Himmler's idealism may have been perverted, increasing rather than reducing human misery, but he was an idealist nonetheless. This unimpressive-looking man combined a cranky interest in herbalism and mysticism with a capacity for phenomenal hard work. He had a ruthless indifference to the suffering of non-Germans, combined with a sense of compassion in other respects. He once insisted on witnessing an SS execution and screamed in horror when two women were not killed instantly. He was appalled by the cruelty of hunting, and he was scrupulously correct in the conduct of his office.

He regarded self-enrichment with disgust, to the amazement of figures like Goering and Robert Ley of the DAF. He insisted on paying for the petrol he consumed when using his staff car to take his elderly parents for a drive. He showed a real concern that the brutal work of the SS should not be morally damaging to his underlings. His hard work, consideration and idealism seem to have engendered a genuine respect within his organisation. Hitler and his circle often privately poked fun at the high seriousness of Himmler, but they valued his loyalty and efficiency.

The 25-year-old Himmler joined the small SS organisation in 1925. This was Hitler's personal bodyguard and a small part of the much larger SA organisation. In 1927 he became its deputy commander, and 2 years later its commander. He spotted its potential. In 1929 it had a strength of 250. By 1931 it was 10,000 strong and in 1933 it had reached 52,000. He also had the ability to spot talented assistants. In 1930 he accepted the services of a young cashiered naval lieutenant, Reinhard Heydrich, as head of the new intelligence unit of the SS. It was named the SD and had a staff of one. Three years later there were 120 agents. Some were later to feel that Heydrich was the real brains of the partnership and the secret behind the expansion of the Himmler empire.

Like many empires it had begun unimpressively. Himmler was appointed head of the political police in Munich in March 1933. He quickly set up a model camp — Dachau, a name that would strike terror into the hearts of many German citizens over the next few years. Once again he showed a talent for spotting deputies when he appointed Theodore Eicke to be the first commandant of this model camp. Later, Eicke was to supervise the multiplying network of terror camps across Germany and eastern Europe.

In April 1933 Himmler became police commander for the whole of Bavaria, the second largest German state. He quickly set his eyes on his next target, Prussia, the largest of the German states, comprising three-fifths of Germany. He skilfully exploited a turf war going on between Goering, the effective head of Prussia, and Wilhelm Frick, Minister of the Interior for the whole of Germany and a man anxious to rationalise Germany's police force under his control. In April 1934 Goering did a deal with Himmler and appointed him head of the Prussian Gestapo in place of Rudolf Diels.

The object was to frustrate Frick's ambitions. In this Goering succeeded, but he lost control of the Gestapo despite the fact that he remained nominally in charge.

Himmler and Goering cooperated further during the Night of the Long Knives, when they both played a part in removing Röhm and his leading SA henchmen. It was Heydrich who supposedly conjured up the evidence necessary to convince Hitler that Röhm was involved in a plot against him.

Himmler received his reward when the SS was established as an independent organisation, free from SA control. In 1936 he achieved his ambition of becoming head of all police forces in every state. He was technically Frick's deputy, but in Nazi Germany the theoretical chain of command was not always the true one. In 1939 he was finally able to coordinate the entire security apparatus under an SS umbrella, the **RHSA**, led by Heydrich. It combined the Gestapo, SD, *Kripo* (criminal police) and the ordinary police. By this time the number of camps had multiplied under another branch of the SS — the death's head detachments. He had also in that year established the Waffen SS, which was to grow into an army under his direct command.

The Gestapo and the SD

Few organisations have acquired such an evil reputation as the political police of Nazi Germany. They were clearly a key element in the repression of opponents of the regime.

The Gestapo of Prussia came under Himmler's control in 1934. They already had wide emergency powers that had been used in 1933 under the first chief, Rudolf Diels. As some semblance of normality returned, it might have been expected that these emergency powers would be curtailed. In fact in 1936 they were made permanent, in effect placing the Gestapo above the law. They could arrest and detain people without trial, and their treatment of prisoners was subject only to their own internal disciplinary proceedings. The Gestapo's very existence and powers added up to a real shift of balance between the rights of the individual and the power of the state, and the shift was very much in favour of the state.

The work of the Gestapo has been the subject of intense historical controversy. Its image as an all-powerful and ubiquitous organisation was deliberately fostered by the regime. This was played up by Allied wartime propaganda, and later it served as an alibi to excuse the behaviour of the German people in accepting Hitler. This viewpoint was well expressed in an early study, *The Gestapo*, by a French historian writing in 1962, Jaques Delarue. He entitled one chapter 'The Gestapo is Everywhere'.

As detailed local research began in the 1970s and 1980s, a different story began to emerge, which might be termed revisionist. The German historians Klaus Mallman and Gerhard Paul published an influential article on the Gestapo satirically entitled 'Omniscient, omnipotent and omnipresent' in 1994. They pointed out that this was not an accurate description.

The Gestapo was overworked and understrength, and far from being composed of fanatical Nazis, it was made up of somewhat under-educated professional police. In fact, the operational head of the Gestapo was a professional policeman, Heinrich Müller, whose lack of good Nazi Party credentials was denounced by the deputy Gauleiter of Munich in 1937.

The American historian Robert Gellately produced a similar picture in his study based on the Gestapo archives of Würzburg and published as *The Gestapo and German Society* by OUP in 1990. Elsewhere in Germany the same picture emerged. Sometimes a Gestapo office consisted of one man. In the bigger cities like Leipzig the number of officers was only 100, and the ratio of Gestapo officers to citizens was roughly one to 10,500 throughout the whole state of Saxony. The Gestapo was clearly not everywhere; officers were usually slaving over a desk dealing with endless paperwork, swamped by demands from Gestapo Central Office in Berlin and handling the wave of denunciations from ordinary Germans of their neighbours. It is this last phenomenon that came to be accepted as the key element of control: ordinary Germans appeared to police themselves. Much of the Gestapo's work was sifting genuine information from the malevolent and malicious.

A study by Eric A. Johnson entitled *Nazi Terror* and published by Basic Books in 1999 has sought to modify the revisionist view. Johnson confirms the size and nature of the Gestapo but points out that most officers were of conservative and right-wing sympathies, even if they were not members of the Nazi Party. He also points to the very efficient conduct of their business, which he claims arose from the simple procedure of targeting. Ordinary Germans were left alone. Communists, Jews and other suspect groups received the full focus of Gestapo energies, and to purposeful effect.

The *Kripo*

The criminal police of Nazi Germany have received less attention. In fact they enjoyed a high profile during the Third Reich, when special 'Days of the German Police' were publicly celebrated. Their powers were considerably extended, summarised in their slogan: 'The fist comes down'. A constant theme of the regime was that life had been too soft for criminals under the Weimar Republic and that now they would get their just deserts. In September 1933 there was a massive crackdown on beggars and vagrants, with as many as 100,000 being picked up by police. Such actions became the subject of extensive propaganda by the regime and appear to have been popular. In November 1933 a new law was decreed against dangerous and habitual criminals. Throughout much of the 1930s there was a constant campaign against 'asocials' — alcoholics, homosexuals and persistent criminals. The laws of evidence were amended to make prosecution easier and many were arrested by police fiat.

The justification was always the public interest, which was seen as superior to the rights of the individual. Hitler himself drove this trend along, urging the torture of a child-murderer in one singular case. Although most judges were left in place, they were under considerable pressure to take a tougher line on criminals. Hitler and

most active members of his party had little sympathy with the finer points of law; they wanted action and in this they probably represented public opinion. Nazi policy with regard to law and order appears to have been massively popular. Hitler embodied the simplistic response of the man in the street: the answer to crime was to get tough. Himmler linked the *Kripo* under Arthur Nebe with the Gestapo under Müller into one body in 1936 — the security police or *Sipo*, under the overall command of Heydrich.

Concentration camps

Perhaps the most infamous and horrific aspect of Nazi Germany was the network of camps that spread across the country to detain dissidents. Himmler probably took seriously his claims that the purpose was to re-educate. Michael Burleigh has chillingly described them as 'the dark side of the moon'. To him their purpose was clear: 'to isolate potential opponents and to break their spirits'. Any reading of Theodore Eicke's rules for the conduct of the first SS concentration camp at Dachau will confirm this judgement. Refusing to work was punishable by death. Making a derogatory remark against the government or leadership was punishable by 2 weeks of confinement, with 25 strokes before the period of confinement and afterwards. Eicke utilised his famous tree hanging to great effect, whereby a prisoner's hands were tied behind his back and then he was hauled up by his hands over the branch of a tree, thereby inflicting excruciating pain and dislocating the shoulders.

In practice, guards were given the powers to terrorise and humiliate prisoners at will. The temporary SA 'wild' camps of 1933 were closed, but the new model SS camps replaced them. Dachau, near Munich, was followed by Sachsenhaussen in 1936 and Buchenwald in 1937. Three more were built in 1938.

These were not extermination camps like those built in the 1940s in Poland. The chief victims were perceived opponents of the regime, mainly Communists and a scattering of Social Democrats. Most were released, broken in spirit as intended. The camps were not secret but in fact became the focus of propaganda by the regime.

The numbers involved as prisoners in these camps is indicative of the degree of terror at any one time. In the course of 1933 perhaps 100,000 Germans were arrested, most being sent to one of the SA wild camps. It is estimated that 500 to 600 died. The vast bulk of detainees were quickly released, many in a Christmas amnesty of 1933. Throughout 1934 more were released and many camps like that at Oranienburg were closed. By the late autumn of 1934 there were fewer than 500 prisoners in all the camps in Prussia and only 1,600 in Bavaria. Throughout the whole of Germany only 3,000 prisoners were being held in camps at the end of the year. The majority appeared to be committed Communists.

It seemed that the regime had acquired a wide body of support, and terror was not needed. There was active discussion about the possible abolition of all camps, but Himmler won Hitler's support for the retention of some at a meeting in June 1935. These were to be used increasingly for 'asocials' as well as committed political opponents. By November 1936 there were 4,761 prisoners, of whom politicals still formed the bulk at 3,694.

From 1937 to the outbreak of war there was a steady rise in the number of inmates. There were 8,000 in 1937 with more 'asocials' supplied by the *Kripo*. As international tension rose and the fear of war grew, many senior Communists were re-arrested. Flossenberg opened in early May 1938 — it was deliberately designed to house the socially undesirable rather than political opponents, and housed 1,500 inmates by 1939. It has been estimated that by the time of the outbreak of war in September 1939, the total camp population had reached 21,400, and it continued to rise thereafter.

Assessment of the role of terror

It is difficult to make an accurate assessment of how important terror was to the new regime. Clearly, as the figures above show, it played some part in 1933. Thereafter it was less important. It was more extensive than the terror operated by Mussolini in Italy, but considerably less brutal and extensive than that of Stalin in Russia, where the camp population exceeded 1 million throughout most of the 1930s.

Historians vary in the emphasis they place upon the terror. Pierre Aycoberry devotes the first chapter of *The Social History of the Third Reich* to it, emphasising its role and importance in the Third Reich. To make such an assessment, much depends upon which groups in German society are considered and at which date. Robert Gellately, in *Backing Hitler* published by The New Press in 2000, reaches the following conclusion:

> In their successful cultivation of popular opinion, the Nazis did not need to use widespread terror against the population to establish the regime. They had little need to use terror as had the makers of the great modern revolutions like those in France, Russia or China... At every level there was much popular support for the expanding missions of the new police and the camps, especially as the latter were presented in the media as boot camps in which the state would confine both political 'criminals' and variously defined asocials, in order to subject them to 'work therapy'.

Given the bitter divisions in German society before the Nazi takeover, the scale of imprisonment and maltreatment of opponents in the 1930s is perhaps less than might be expected from a regime that made such a cult of violence and hatred. It does appear to have achieved remarkable consensual support from the German people. Violence was an ingredient in this support, but not perhaps the vital one. To play down the role of terror in the 1930s is not, however, to understate the horrific and obscene atrocities of the 1940s — the structures that would be responsible for these atrocities were already in place in 1939.

Glossary and concepts

RHSA — Reich Security Main Office, established in September 1939 on Himmler's orders to coordinate all security police work under Heydrich.

Goebbels and propaganda

Josef Goebbels

'We drive to see Hitler...He's glad to see me. I am in heaven. That man has got everything to be a King.' So recorded Goebbels in his diary. He appears to have genuinely worshipped Hitler. Unlike many of the Nazi leaders, he was personally close to the Führer and frequently shared the rather dull fare at Hitler's table. Although he had been pronounced unfit for war service, this intelligent man played a major part in shaping the Hitler myth and bringing the Third Reich into existence.

Coming from a working-class, Catholic background, at a time when only the middle and upper classes attended university, the young Josef achieved a doctorate in philology in 1921. He was a devoted nationalist but also a sympathiser with the Bolshevik Revolution, a sympathy never completely lost. He was always a radical seeking to transform Germany into a more egalitarian society. He appears to have had far more sympathy for Soviet Russia than for what he perceived to have been the decadent, capitalist West. His conception of National Socialism was probably closest to Hitler's. The two of them poked fun at Himmler and Rosenberg for their heavy-handed fanaticism.

Like Hitler, Goebbels had at heart a contempt for humanity. Like so many of his generation, the generation that Nietzsche wrote for, he recognised the moral hole at the heart of European civilisation. He had lost his faith in religion but he discovered Hitler and the power of theatre: presentation was everything, and illusion could substitute for reality. Perhaps there was nothing to believe in, but human beings could still make a great show of their lives. He was fascinated by films and their power to create illusions in which the masses could lose themselves. Perhaps the whole of the Third Reich should be seen as a gigantic piece of the theatre, essentially meaningless but memorable. In this sense Hitler and Goebbels achieved their objective as the number of children and students studying the Third Reich bear testimony, 50 years after its dramatic theatrical collapse. Hitler, with Goebbels' assistance, re-enacted Wagner for real and the ruined shell of Berlin was a stage setting for the ultimate perfomance of Götterdämmerung. The millions of corpses were film extras and Goebbels would be happy to think of himself as collecting an Oscar for best supporting actor.

As director of party propaganda he played a major part in boosting its support. He had taken charge of the breakthrough election of 1930, and thereafter carefully stage-managed the presentation of Hitler and the party to Germany. When the Nazis came to power he was brought into the government in March 1933 as head of a new Ministry of Propaganda and Public Enlightenment. His task was to sell the new regime to Germany and to make possible the National Awakening. He rapidly built up an empire to rival that of the other Nazi chieftains. He saw his chief rivals as Alfred Rosenberg, the party expert on culture and ideology, and Max Amann, Hitler's old sergeant from the First World War and now the head of an expanding Nazi publishing empire.

Like all the other successful Nazi leaders, Goebbels' success relied on a combination of talent, sharp elbows and above all proximity to Hitler.

The press

To the new minister, the press was the least important and least interesting of the areas to be controlled. The written word was regarded as less powerful than the spoken word. Germany had a vast number of newspapers, and even small towns might boast two or three of their own. Very few had large circulations and most were local. There were no equivalents to the great national newspapers that existed in Britain.

From 1933 a complex system of control evolved. In part this system grew up as a result of the rivalry between Goebbels and Max Amann. Goebbels sought to control the press through the journalists and editors, whilst Amann sought control of the publishers. Both succeeded, giving the Nazis a double stranglehold on the press.

Max Amann was elected chairman of the German Publishers Association in June 1933. In November 1933 he became president at the Reich Press Chamber, membership of which was obligatory for anyone wishing to publish a newspaper. Over the next few years, hundreds of papers were closed or taken over by Amann's Nazi publishing empire, even though the original names were often kept and the public were unaware of the changed ownership. By 1939 his organisation, Eher Verlag, controlled two-thirds of the German press. At the same time there was a massive boost in circulation of the *Volkischer Beobachter*, the official Nazi newspaper. It was the first German newspaper to reach a circulation of a million, largely because officials of all sorts — school teachers, civil servants and university professors — felt obliged to buy a copy and display it. Teachers were particularly worried that pupils might copy out sections of this official Nazi paper in their work and then receive derogatory comments on it. Such a mistake would not only be bad for the teacher's career but could also bring physical danger.

At the same time as Amann was enhancing his control of publishing, Goebbels and his deputy Otto Dietrich, the Nazi press chief, were extending their control over editors and journalists. All the journalists had to be members of the Reich Association of the German Press. In October 1933 Goebbels won a victory over Amann which gave considerable powers to the editor as opposed to the owner of a newspaper. It was the editors who were responsible for the content of the papers and they were made subject to self-censorship. The ministry also sought to control the papers through a state monopoly of news provision by setting up the DNB (German news bureau). There were daily briefings too as to what could and could not be printed, the latter often including the most trivial incidents. Anything that might cast senior Nazi figures in a bad light was removed from the press.

The end product was tame, and even Goebbels admitted it was a remarkably boring collection of newspapers. The standard text on this is *The Captive Press* by Oron J. Hale, published by Princeton in 1964. There are shorter but excellent summaries in

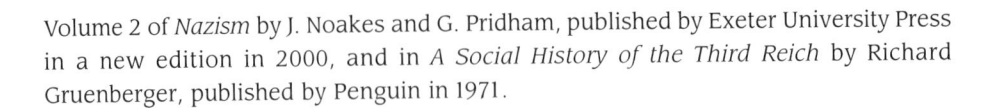

Volume 2 of *Nazism* by J. Noakes and G. Pridham, published by Exeter University Press in a new edition in 2000, and in *A Social History of the Third Reich* by Richard Gruenberger, published by Penguin in 1971.

Radio

Radio was of much greater interest to the new Minister of Propaganda. His first battle was to create a national network, wresting control from individual states. The local Gauleiter were reluctant to hand control to Berlin, but with Hitler's backing Goebbels succeeded and in April 1934 the Reich Radio Company was set up under the control of Goebbels' ministry. There was a major purge of broadcasting staff, with 13% being dismissed — mainly those who were Jewish or of left-wing sympathies.

Over the next few years there was a massive drive to increase the ownership of radios. A new, inexpensive model was produced, which had the additional advantage of not being able to tune in to foreign stations. By 1939 perhaps 70% of all Germans had access to private radios, one of the highest percentages in the world. Before this was achieved there had been a policy of encouraging public access by placing radios in cafés and public places. Hitler frequently broadcast in the early days of the regime, as did Goebbels, giving rise to the joke that a 'goeb' was the unit of electrical power needed to switch off 100,000 receivers.

Film

Film was the new minister's greatest love. He was fascinated by this new medium, which had the added attraction of bringing him into contact with a stream of young starlets. Many of these later recorded the remarkable charm he had, but it was of course a charm wedded to considerable powers of patronage that could make or break a young actor. There was an average output of around 100 films a year during the Third Reich.

Goebbels' view of film was quite different from that of Hitler. While the Führer preferred direct propaganda, the Minister of Propaganda wanted entertainment. As one commentator put it, he wanted to poison with a sugared pill. More than anything, he required films to be entertaining. He wanted the audience to seek out the film and to come out feeling good. The result was a series of costume dramas and light-hearted song and dance movies — he hated obvious propaganda films like *Hitlerjunge Quex*. The most famous propaganda films of the Third Reich were not his work but that of the young independent film director, Leni Riefenstahl. In making her two famous films *The Triumph of the Will* and *Olympia* she was acting directly under Hitler's orders, and Goebbels was jealous of her access to the boss. Goebbels preferred films in which Hitler was portrayed not as himself but indirectly as one of Germany's heroes from the past, such as Frederick the Great. Goebbels understood how important it was not to over-expose your star. He deliberately created and played upon the image of Hitler as a remote, god-like figure watching over Germany and denying himself the comforts of life. As an image it appears to have been triumphantly successful, and Hitler appreciated the importance of Goebbels' work.

Ritual and rallies

Just as in its politics National Socialism sought to combine left and right, so in its presentation of itself it sought to use the new world of radio and film but also appreciated the value of a religious-style ritual reminiscent of the Middle Ages.

Few things better illustrate the fact that National Socialism was a religion invented for the twentieth century than its ritual. A new round of 'holy days' was set up — the celebration of the seizure of power on 30 January, Hero Remembrance Day in March, Hitler's birthday on 20 April, the Day of Labour on 1 May, Mother's Day in June, the commemoration of the failed Munich putsch on 9 November with its relic of the bloody flag — all these invited worship and involvement.

A new meaning was to be given to life in the Third Reich. In every town rallies and processions demanded the attention and involvement of the citizens to demonstrate a commitment to a new world. The greatest of these was of course the Nuremberg rally, held in the autumn every year. From all over Germany nearly half a million poured into the city of Nuremberg to celebrate the rebirth of Germany and hear the Führer for themselves. This clearly played a major part in drawing Germany together. It should not be forgotten that a third of Germans were rural peasants and unused to long-distance travel, and rallies such as this created a sense of national identity. Even those who could not attend could witness the scenes of national commitment on the cinema screen or listen to speeches on the ubiquitous radios.

The key aim in all of this was to create a sense of belonging and unity in the *Volksgemeinschaft*. Its appeal was all the more powerful in the light of the bitter divisions and social problems of 1929–32. Ultimately it appealed to the fundamental human need to worship and belong, which Goebbels and the Nazi Party exploited.

Goering and the economy

Hermann Goering

'I have no conscience, Adolf Hitler is my conscience.' So said the iron man of the Nazi movement, and in many ways the most successful of Nazi chieftains in the 1930s. By 1939 he was Hitler's designated successor and had acquired more offices and power than anyone else. He had been one of the original cabinet members in 1933, with crucial control of the Prussian police, which played such a large part in the consolidation of power. Thereafter he supervised the Gestapo, and in the role of Minister of the Interior of Prussia he set up and controlled the *Forschungsamt*, a sophisticated information-gathering service relying on telephone taps and every form of eavesdropping.

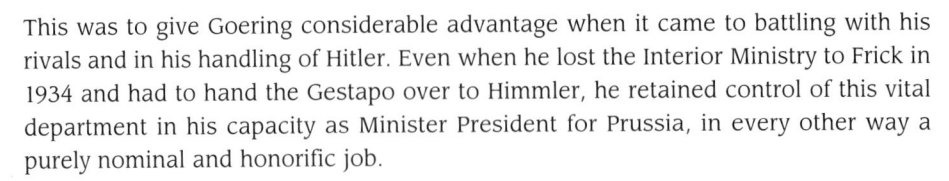

This was to give Goering considerable advantage when it came to battling with his rivals and in his handling of Hitler. Even when he lost the Interior Ministry to Frick in 1934 and had to hand the Gestapo over to Himmler, he retained control of this vital department in his capacity as Minister President for Prussia, in every other way a purely nominal and honorific job.

In May 1933, against the bitter opposition of the army and General von Blomberg, he gained control of the new Air Ministry. He was able to win complete independence for this in 1934. The Night of the Long Knives of that year removed a dangerous rival in Röhm, but he felt curiously frustrated at the end of the year. He enjoyed great prestige and was probably the best-known Nazi figure after Hitler, but apart from the Air Ministry, which he ran through deputies, he held no senior party jobs.

Like all the leading Nazis, the roots of his power lay in his connection with Hitler. The connection went back to 1922, and there appears to have been a genuine bond of loyalty, although not of affection, between them. They were never personally close and Hitler always addressed Goering as *Sie*, not *du*. Goering was always in awe of his chief and genuinely revered him as the leader. Hitler appreciated Goering's energy and the ice-cold determination he showed in crisis after crisis. After their many formal meetings Hitler used to say that he felt as if he had 'bathed in steel'.

Goering was quite different from the other leaders. He came from an upper-class background and had been a First World War hero, commanding the famous Red Baron's fighter squadron after the Red Baron had been shot down. He was a man fizzing with energy and possessed of a bright if untutored intelligence. He loved action and had little time for ideas. He frequently dismissed ideology and seems to have felt little genuine anti-Semitism. He had been brought up by a Jewish stepfather, for whom he had real affection. Yet there was a total lack of morality and a cold determination in his nature.

He exploited his positions to enrich himself and his family. He loved display and was famous for his gaudy uniforms, which he often changed four times a day, to the amusement of the German public and the contempt of his associates. He appears to have been genuinely popular with the public, who seem to have regarded him as fat, funny and approachable, in marked contrast to Hitler. There were more jokes told about him than anyone else and he loved collecting and retelling them.

Hitler did not enjoy the duties of his social role as head of the Reich and he often left this function to Goering. The result was that a series of high-profile social events starred this larger-than-life figure.

The four-year plan, 1936–37

Goering skilfully exploited the growing economic crisis of 1935–36 to enhance his position and massively extend his empire. The rapid rearmament was causing real problems for the Minister of Economics, Schacht. There was the threat of inflation, a balance of payments crisis and food shortages in the cities. Schacht's answer was simple — to slow down the rearmament programme and boost exports. This brought him into conflict with the army, and was certainly not what Hitler wanted. The key issue was the import of those raw materials in which Germany was not self-sufficient. Oil was clearly of vital importance, particularly to the new German air force and its chief.

Throughout the spring and summer of 1936, Goering and Hitler worked closely together to try to solve the problem of raw materials, and the answer appeared to be greater self-sufficiency. This involved exploiting Germany's raw materials and cutting down on imports. Synthetic oil could be made from coal but at great cost, and Germany could be rendered less dependent on imports of iron ore from Sweden if low-grade German ores were used, again at great cost.

The result was the establishment of the four-year plan with Goering at its head. It was announced at the Nuremberg rally of 1936, and made Goering the second most important person in the Reich. He used it brilliantly to push aside rivals and expand his power base. Two ministries in particular suffered, as well as that of Economics. He simply drafted the senior civil servants of the ministries of Labour and Agriculture into the four-year plan organisation, leaving these men's nominal superiors high and dry. Schacht fought back, but as Goering took more and more decisions away from his ministry he eventually resigned in 1937, to be replaced by Goering's henchman Walter Funk.

Goering was now the effective head of the whole German economy. The four-year plan organisation became a vast bureaucracy and the Hermann Goering steelworks was the biggest industrial enterprise in Europe. The 'presents' that came to Goering from German industry massively inflated his wealth, an example of corruption to which Hitler turned a blind eye.

The Blomberg–Fritsch Affair, 1938

Goering now sought to control the entire rearmament programme, but standing in the way was General von Blomberg of the Ministry of War. The removal of Blomberg and Werner von Fritsch, the commander-in-chief of the army, was a murky and mysterious story of double-dealing and opportunism, skills in which Goering excelled.

In November 1937, Hitler faced demands from the armed services for a clear statement of priorities in the allocation of steel and raw materials. This led to a conference in November, known to historians from the memo which describes it as the Hossbach conference. Typically, Hitler refused to make a clear-cut decision and simply launched into a general situation report in which he described the likelihood of war. Blomberg and von Fritsch were horrified as the army was not ready, and made their opposition clear to Hitler.

Early in 1938 the 59-year-old Blomberg remarried, to a woman in her twenties of much lower social standing. The marriage was encouraged by Goering and it seemed to fit the National Socialist ideal of a classless society. The woman, however, was of even lower social standing than Blomberg realised — she was a part-time prostitute who had posed for pornographic photos. Evidence was provided by Himmler's organisation and Goering went to Hitler with the news. Blomberg had to resign in February 1938. Meanwhile Himmler's organisation had dredged up a homosexual scandal allegedly involving von Fritsch, and this led to his resignation.

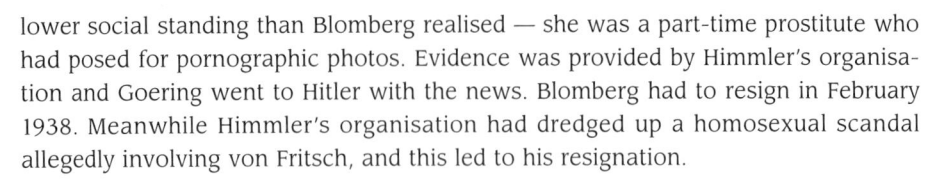

Two obstacles to a more radical foreign policy had been removed and Hitler was grateful, although not so grateful as to make Goering Minister of War, a post he felt he was unfit for. He was, however, promoted to Field Marshal, making him the highest-ranking officer in Germany. Hitler himself became Minister of War, so Goering could not feel slighted. Goering's prestige had been increased but not his real power. The whole episode illustrates the complex infighting that was characteristic of high-level politics in the Third Reich.

Living standards — winners and losers

In judging popular responses to the Third Reich, its effect on living standards and quality of life must be assessed. This is clearly a complex process and as in all societies there were winners and losers. At one extreme were Germany's Jewish citizens, increasingly marginalised and driven to emigration. At the other extreme were the 'golden pheasants', as the party big bosses were known. No pheasant was more golden then Goering. In between these two extremes, generalisations become more difficult and have occasioned controversy amongst historians.

In general, Marxist historians such as T. W. Mason have seen the workers as losers, kept in place by repression and propaganda, but although there was repression, this is too simple. To the unemployed of 1932, the Third Reich brought prosperity of a kind, for by 1939 there was full employment and real labour shortages. There had been the benefits also, perhaps more promised than delivered, of improved working conditions brought about by the DAF, and the prospect of exciting holidays organised through the KdF movement (*Kraft durch Freude*, or 'Strength through Joy', the National Socialist leisure organisation). Perhaps it was only a minority who truly benefited, but the prospect of benefits was used fully in government propaganda.

It can be argued that the increased job opportunities and security had to be balanced against longer hours of work and less freedom. In some ways the diets of working-class families deteriorated, with greater consumption of rye bread, produced from home-grown grain, as opposed to the more expensive white or wheat bread, produced from imports. Tropical fruits were in short supply and the consumption of beer fell. On the other hand, more Germans attended the cinema and possessed a radio.

For the middle classes there was a similar mixture of gains and losses. Perhaps the biggest gains were security from the Communist menace and a declining crime rate. It seemed safer to walk the streets; if one toed the party line there was job security and comfort of a sort. Presumably, the pressure to conform, the monotony of endless party parades and the harassment for donations to winter relief charities may have been resented.

Among industrialists, there were winners and losers too. Some companies like IG Farben were enormous winners, with vast contracts and enhanced profits. Others, like the steel manufacturers that refused to cooperate with Goering's four-year plan, tended to lose out. For all manufacturers, there was the benefit that came from a labour force without independent trade unions, but there was a meddling bureaucracy and a vastly increased amount of form filling.

The new DAF organisation did tend to insist on job security for the workers and in this sense did fulfil part of the role of the trade unions, and it had teeth. Ulrich Herbert, in an essay entitled 'Good times, bad times: memories of the Third Reich' in *Life in the Third Reich*, edited by Richard Bessel and published by OUP in 1987, summarises the situation as follows:

> *All politics aside, for a large part of the population the image of National Socialism was characterised principally not by terror, mass murder and war, but by reduction of unemployment, economic boom, tranquillity and order.*

Ian Kershaw tends to agree with this judgement in a paper published in German in 1985. He notes:

> *…the ability of the regime before the war to improve considerably the living standards of almost all sectors of the population in comparison to the period of the world economic crisis — or at least raise hopes of an imminent improvement.*

These views must be borne in mind when considering the extent of opposition to the regime.

Opposition and resistance

Like all aspects of Nazi Germany, the extent and role of opposition to Nazism has been the subject of bitter controversy amongst historians. As always the division goes back to the Marxist/East German interpretation and the West German or liberal/conservative view. Marxist historians and those on the left of the political spectrum have tended to emphasise the role of the working class in resisting the Nazi regime and seen the Communist Party as the heroes of the struggle. They tend to downplay the resistance of the churches, the old élite and the army. By comparison, liberal/conservative historians have played up the role of the churches, the old élite and the army and seen the Communists as at best irrelevant and in some ways as unwitting allies of the Nazis.

As well as this ideological divide between historians, there is methodological division. The 1970s and 1980s saw a growth in the study of the history of ordinary people and attempts to measure their responses. In a sense this was history from the bottom up rather than the top down. A massive study of popular attitudes and behaviour in Bavaria was supervised by the eminent German historian Martin Broszat. He emphasised the role of non-conformity, *Resistenz* in German, as opposed to the more dangerous forms of opposition that would be termed 'resistance'. This concept sparked off a major debate as to the importance of such non-conformity. Many questioned the importance given to it by Broszat.

The most critical were two German historians who had studied the Gestapo in the Saarland, Klaus Mallmann and Gerhard Paul. A good introduction to the historiography of this subject is in Chapter 3 of Ian Kershaw's *The Nazi Dictatorship: Problems and Perspectives of Interpretation*, published by Arnold in 1993 (3rd edition). In the same year *Inside Nazi Germany* by Detlev Peukert appeared, a study of conformity and opposition. An excellent collection of documents edited by Martyn Housden was published in 1997, and a brief introduction to this whole topic is provided in a pamphlet by Frank McDonough: *Opposition and Resistance in Nazi Germany*, published by CUP in 2001. This, like all the books on this topic, covers the whole period 1933–45, with the bulk of the coverage relating to the war years, which are not part of this specification.

The workers and the political left

The Social Democratic Party had a million members in 1933 and the Communist Party had over 300,000. It might be expected that these two groups would put up considerable resistance to the Nazi regime. What is extraordinary is the speed with which they were crushed in 1933 and their lack of effective resistance over the next 6 years.

Thousands were arrested and hundreds killed in 1933 but by the end of the year, as indicated on page 30, large numbers were being released. The SPD leadership went into exile and attempted to set up an underground network for resistance. In 1933 they established the newspaper *Red Shock Troop*, based in Berlin, but this was broken up by the Gestapo in December of that year. Another underground newspaper, *Socialist Action*, was set up, but in January 1935 the Gestapo arrested the leaders.

The SPD became increasingly disillusioned. It produced a series of reports on the popularity of the regime, and the chances of effective resistance. These 'SOPADE' reports are of considerable use to historians but, as indicated on page 7, they tend to be rather pessimistic about the chances of effective resistance.

Communists suffered much more from repression and never really recovered from the initial onslaught of 1933. In 1935 the Gestapo estimated that 5,000 Communist members were active in resistance in Berlin. In the larger cities of Berlin and Hamburg the Communist resistance could hope to continue. A spate of pamphlets was produced, with 1.2 million in 1934 alone. Large numbers of activists were rounded up by the Gestapo, however, and the best that could be hoped for was the survival of a skeleton organisation. Many showed great courage in resisting what they perceived as a tyranny, but they were in fact the servants of a regime in Moscow which at the time was an even worse tyranny.

The two leading left-wing parties, then, largely failed to produce effective resistance. The bitter division between the two groups partly accounts for their weakness. On the left of the Social Democratic Party a small group saw disunity as the problem and formed an organisation, New Beginning. It too was broken up by the Gestapo with a series of arrests in 1935 and again in 1938. Repression clearly played a part in containing the working class, but it does appear that the regime gained the support of a considerable portion of workers with its successes in foreign policy and in reducing unemployment. As Alf Ludtke wrote in his essay 'German workers and the limits of resistance', published in 1992 and reprinted in *The Third Reich* edited by C. Leitz, Blackwell, 1999:

> For the most part, workers did not keep their distance from the cheering masses. They joined them, for instance, at the Nazi May Day of National Labour, or when Hitler's voice was heard on the radio, or in the newsreel celebrating another 'great day' in the nation's history.

The role of the churches

The majority of Germans belonged to the Protestant, or as it was often known the Evangelical, Church. They faced a serious attempt by the regime to establish effective ideological control through a single Reich Church under Bishop Ludwig Müller. In December 1933 he amalgamated the Evangelical Youth with the Hitler Youth. There was, however, stiff resistance to further control.

In the vanguard of the fight was an organisation set up in September 1933, the Confessing Church led by an ex-U-boat captain and undoubted conservative patriot, Rev. Martin Niemöller. Despite extensive Gestapo harassment, the Confessing Church defeated the attempts to control worship and Hitler abandoned Müller's Reich Church in 1937, to the annoyance of Nazi fanatics like Bormann. However, Niemöller and many of the other Confessing Church pastors were sent to camps. The regime had suffered a defeat but was not threatened.

The Roman Catholic Church had signed a deal with the regime in July 1933, the Concordat, dissolving the Catholic Centre Party in return for independence in religious matters. Over the next few years, priests faced harassment in some areas from zealous local Nazis seeking to remove crucifixes from churches and to stop Catholic Youth movements. The Catholics resisted effectively but their resentment never developed into political opposition to the regime, whose legitimacy the Catholic hierarchy never challenged. The Catholic Church nevertheless defended its own independence and after 1939 effectively opposed, eventually, the murder of the disabled.

The army

The one institution that could threaten Nazism, and perhaps came closest to overthrowing Hitler in September 1938, was the German army. Many army officers, like the commander-in-chief in 1933, General von Hammerstein-Equord, disliked the Nazis intensely and openly referred to them as 'that gang of criminals'. By 1938 there was sufficient concern about Hitler's intention to drag Germany into another war that an extensive conspiracy of senior army officers and conservative politicians, such as

Schacht and Karl Goerdeler (the ex-mayor of Leipzig and, like Schacht, an ex-minister in Hitler's government), resolved on a coup the moment the expected war over Czechoslovakia broke out. It involved senior figures in the Foreign Office (who hated their new Nazi boss, von Ribbentrop) and Hans Oster, a senior figure in the military intelligence service, the *Abwehr*.

The key players were the ex-chief of the army general staff, General Ludwig Beck, and his replacement Franz Halder, who referred to his Führer as 'mentally ill'. The commander of the Berlin military district was involved and also the aristocratic commander of the crack Potsdam division, who had the detailed points of the coup worked out and checked by 14 September. The plotters were unsure what to do with Hitler. They were very conscious of his popularity, and Halder could not bring himself to contemplate murder. As it happened they never had to face the decision. The Munich Conference at the end of the month avoided war but brought Hitler enhanced prestige. The opportunity passed.

Resistenz (non-conformity)

Clearly, as in all societies, there were dissidents in Nazi Germany who rejected what was officially approved, and embraced a counter-culture. Perhaps the most widely known form of non-conformity was the 'swing-kids' movement that developed at the end of the 1930s in big cities like Hamburg. This involved youngsters in their teens who rejected the Hitler Youth, wore long hair and jitterbugged to the sound of American and British big bands or listened to jazz. They endured intermittent persecution but they hardly threatened the regime's stability. With regard to non-conformity as a whole, it is difficult to disagree with Ian Kershaw's judgement that 'for the functioning of the regime the large spheres of consensus were undoubtedly much more important than the areas of dissent'.

Assessment

It is hard to resist the conclusion that Hitler largely succeeded in creating consent. There was to be no 'stab in the back'. A judicious mixture of terror, effective propaganda and genuinely popular policies persuaded Germans not only to tolerate the Nazis but, in large numbers, to give enthusiastic support. As Ian Kershaw wrote in his paper on resistance in 1985:

> Not only did the resistance to Hitler act without the active mass support of the population, but, down to the end, large proportions of the population did not passively support the resistance, but actually widely condemned it.

Questions & Answers

In this section there are five specimen exam questions. They illustrate the range and type of source extracts you will come across.

Two specimen answers are given to each exam question. One of these is an A-grade answer, but examples of lower-grade answers are included to point out common errors — either in approach or in exam technique.

All the specimen answers are the subject of detailed examiner comments, preceded by the icon ℮. These should be studied carefully as they show how and why marks are awarded or lost. The A-grade answers demonstrate common features such as:
- the appropriate use of outside knowledge to put source material in context
- a clear and persistent focus on answering the question asked
- a structured and logical approach
- an apportionment of time and effort appropriate to marks that can be gained in different parts of the question

When exam papers are marked, all answers are given a level of response and then a precise numerical mark. Answers to questions worth 10 marks are normally marked to three levels:
- **level 1:** 1–3 marks
- **level 2:** 4–7 marks
- **level 3:** 8–10 marks

The final essay is marked to four levels:
- **level 1:** 1–5 marks, involves very simple statements and the use of either own knowledge or information from one extract
- **level 2:** 6–10 marks, involves either own knowledge and limited source use, or excellent use of the sources alone, or excellent own knowledge
- **level 3:** 11–16 marks, involves using both sources and own knowledge with real focus on the question asked
- **level 4:** 17–20 marks, involves a sustained argument from both the sources and own knowledge

Question 1

(a) Using Sources 1, 2 and 3 and your own knowledge, assess who was responsible for the Night of the Long Knives. (10 marks)

(b) Using your own knowledge and all the sources, assess the role of violence in the Nazi consolidation of power, March 1933–August 1934. (20 marks)

Source 1: *From* The German Army, *M. Cooper, 1978*

The events of the 30 June achieved many goals. The SA, although it remained a large party organisation, was rendered politically and militarily impotent; Hitler's authority was extended; Goering was satisfied at the removal of a rival; Himmler was left free to develop his SS empire; and the Army was confirmed in its position as sole arms-bearer in the defence of the nation. On the 13 July Hitler announced: 'My promise to him [von Hindenburg] to preserve the Army as a non-political instrument of the nation is as binding for me from innermost conviction as from my pledged word.'

Source 2: *From Report on Cabinet Meeting, July 1934*

At the meeting of the Reich Cabinet on Tuesday 3rd July, the Reich Chancellor, Adolf Hitler, began by giving a detailed account of the origin and suppression of the high treason plot. The Reich Chancellor stressed that lightning action had been necessary, otherwise many thousands of people would have been in danger of being wiped out. Defence Minister General von Blomberg thanked the Führer in the name of the Reich Cabinet and the army for his determined and courageous action, by which he had saved the German people from civil war. The Führer had shown greatness as a statesman and soldier. This had aroused in the hearts of the members of the Cabinet and the whole German people a vow of service, devotion, and loyalty in this grave hour.

The Reich Cabinet then approved a law on measures for the self-defence of the State. Its single paragraph reads:

'The measures taken on 30th June and 1st and 2nd July to suppress the acts of high treason are legal, being necessary for the self-defence of the State.'

Reich Minister of Justice Dr Gurtner commented that measures of self-defence taken before the imminent occurrence of a treasonable action should be considered not only legal, but the duty of a statesman.

Source 3: *From* Hitler, 1889–1936: Hubris, *I. Kershaw, 1998*

Röhm's adjutant was ordered by telephone to ensure that all SA leaders attended a meeting with Hitler in Bad Wiessee on the late morning of 30th June. In the meantime, the army had been put on alert. Goering flew back to Berlin to take charge of matters there, ready at a word to move against not only the SA, but also the Papen group. Hitler travelled to Bad Godesberg on the afternoon of 29th June, to be joined in the Rheinhotel Dreesen by Goebbels and Sepp Dietrich, flying in from Berlin. Goebbels had been impatient at Hitler's delay in dealing with the 'reaction' (conservatives). He flew to Godesberg thinking that the strike against Papen and his cronies was finally going to take place. Only on arrival did he learn the main target was Röhm's SA. Hitler reported to him how serious the situation was. There was proof, he claimed (and evidently believed), that Röhm had conspired with the French ambassador François-Poncet, Schleicher and Strasser. So he was determined to act the very next day 'against Röhm and his rebels'. Blood would be shed. They would realise that people lose their heads through rebellion. While arrangements were made, total secrecy had to be maintained.

Source 4: *From* The Social History of the Third Reich, *P. Ayconberry, 1998*

Herman Goering as minister of the interior in East Prussia engaged several thousand SA members as 'auxiliary policemen'. It was a pseudo-regularization that revealed the strategy of the authorities: namely to give free rein to instincts of violence, to protect the perpetrators from any intervention on the part of the last remaining defenders of the law; then to bring them to heel once their principal opponents had been destroyed. While the anti-Communist struggle fell mainly to the regular police, the SA specialized in attacking first Socialist militants, then, in May, trade unionists. There were many old scores to be settled between the mandarins of the moderate Left, formerly pillars of the Republic and longstanding masters of the Prussian police, and their street-brawling opponents. And settled they were: by arrests, torture in places known as 'wild concentration camps,' and assassinations. The lists of adversaries to be struck down included Catholic militants here, Poles there, depending on the region. The case of the Jews demonstrates the extent to which the SA was manipulated by political authorities: it was purely on Goering's initiative that on 10 March they began to harass Jewish people and destroy or confiscate their possessions, thereby providing Goebbels with the pretext for the boycott of 1 April, offcially presented as being 'born out of popular anger'.

Source 5: *From* The Diary of Victor Klemperer *(a Jewish Professor)*

12th April 1933, Wednesday evening
In the afternoon — nice walk, but heart trouble — alone to the Dolzschen council office. To ask them to divide the sewer drain costs (340M) into instalments. Six instalments granted. Up there the Social Democrat mayor has been suspended. I was

received by the commissioner (a giant of a man, with goatee) and the barrel-shaped council surveyor, both in SA uniform. The first time that I've dealt with such people. Both *very* polite, the commissioner a little reserved, visibly anxious about his dignity, the fat one a very homely Saxon, right away chatting to me about the University and the Teacher Training Institute — I must emphasise once again: both uncommonly polite. But here I saw for the first time with my own eyes that we really are entirely at the mercy of the Party dictatorship, of the 'Third Reich', that the Party no longer makes any secret of its absolute power.

And every day new abominations. A Jewish lawyer in Chemnitz kidnapped and shot. 'Provocateurs in SA uniform, common criminals.' Provision of the Civil Service Law. Anyone who has one Jewish grandparent is a Jew. 'In case of doubt the final decision lies with the Specialist for Radical Research in the Reich Interior Ministry.' A worker or employee who is not nationally minded can be dismissed in any factory, [and] must be replaced by a nationally minded one. The NS plant cells must be consulted. Etc. etc. For the moment I am still safe. But as someone on the gallows, who has the rope around his neck, is safe. At any moment a new 'law' can kick away the steps on which I'm standing and then I'm hanging.

Source 6: *From* The Nazi Seizure of Power: The Experience of a Single German Town, *W. S. Allen, 1965*

If enthusiasm was not voluntarily forthcoming, there were other means of evoking it. Of course the blacklisting of former Socialists from employment possibilities continued well into 1934, but that was through behind-the-scenes activity by Girmann [local Nazi leader]. The examples, however, remained as reminders. The most effective means of evoking external compliance was the continued system of terror. Even in the late summer of 1933 there were still arrests to be made, mostly for very minor offenses. Thus in late August it was reported that after a worker had shouted 'Heil Moskau!' he had been sent to the Moringen concentration camp. Reports of similar arrests continued to trickle out. In September a worker was arrested for 'making anti-governmental utterances'. In November 1933, two Northeim women were arrested 'for spreading false rumors about the NSDAP'. But eventually there were no more reports of arrests or other police action. As in other matters, the terror system was stabilizing itself. In September the NNN [local newspaper] felt it advisable to publish an editorial against anonymous denunciations. Perhaps the last public manifestation of Nazi power came in September 1933, when the SA and SS carried out a roundup of beggars in Northeim. It was fruitless, but shortly thereafter the police conducted a similar action and managed to catch one unfortunate victim.

Thus many factors combined to make Nazism a possibility for Northeim. At the same time the town itself influenced the nature of Nazism as it manifested itself locally. It seems probable, for example, that the general lack of violence during the first months of the Third Reich was due to the nature of Northeim as a small town. Much as the Nazis hated all that the Socialists stood for, both sides knew each other too well for cold and systematic violence to occur. The SA might be willing to pummel their neighbors in a street fight, but they seemed to shrink from attacking the Socialists when they were defenseless. This is not to say that no violence took place, but it does help explain the fact that no one was killed and very few were sent to a concentration camp from Northeim during the early years of the Nazi regime.

■ ■ ■

Answer to question 1: A-grade candidate

(a) As all-powerful leader of the Nazis, Hitler was ultimately responsible for whatever took place. As Source 2 shows, he did actually take responsibility for the Night of the Long Knives in front of the Reich Cabinet. Hitler also benefited, as Source 1 tells us that his 'authority was extended': he had got rid of a potential rival. However, Source 1 also shows us that other parties benefited from the event. Goering 'was satisfied at the removal of a rival' and Himmler was no longer subordinate to the SA leader, and so was free to 'develop his SS empire'. The army was secure in its position as the 'sole arms-bearer'. It would be naive to imagine that these groups hadn't tried to influence Hitler to get rid of Röhm. How much effect had their pressure had?

Looking at Source 3 makes the situation even more complex, because it appears that the initial target of the Night of the Long Knives wasn't even Röhm, but 'the Papen group'. The Papen group was a conservative group based in the Chancellery around von Papen and Edgar Jung. They were trying to persuade President Hindenburg that the SA was so dangerous that he must impose martial law, hence removing Hitler, and put themselves in control. Papen's critical Marbug Speech on 17 June precipitated the action against them. On 29 July, as Source 3 tells us, Goebbels thought that the attack was against only the Papen group. Hitler seemed to make the decision to include Röhm in the strike only at the last minute.

Was it at the army's insistence that Hitler turned on the SA? There had been earlier problems. Röhm's aspirations to merge the army and the SA under his own control had considerably disquieted the army élite. Source 2 shows us how grateful General von Blomberg was towards Hitler. However, earlier actions taken showed that Hitler was using other methods to deal with Röhm. The gentlemen's agreement made between Hitler and the army generals had not been specific. Hitler had started cutting down the SA role. By summer 1933 they were no longer auxiliary police in Prussia and by that year's October they had lost control of the concentration camps.

Edexcel Unit 6

Röhm has sometimes been considered responsible for his fate, supposedly challenging Hitler. However, at Hitler's request Röhm had actually sent the SA on leave for the month of July 1934. The idea of a Röhm putsch came from other quarters.

Source 3 seems to hold the answer. Goering is very involved. Goering 'flew back to Berlin to take charge of matters there.' It was Goering and Himmler who had drawn up the death lists for the Night of the Long Knives, and Himmler's SS who had carried out the killings. Certainly this may just have been at Hitler's orders, but their role seems deeper. By the time Goebbels reaches Hitler, Source 3 shows us that Hitler has been convinced by someone that Röhm has turned against him. 'There was proof, he claimed (and evidently believed).' This 'proof' had been dug up by Himmler's SS.

In conclusion, Hitler had a situation to deal with between the SA and the army which he was slowly sorting out. The confrontation with Papen arose, and Himmler and Goering took advantage of this heightened alert situation to turn Hitler on Röhm as well. It had not been Hitler's original intention.

e This is an excellent answer that uses the sources and sets them in the context of considerable 'own knowledge' to produce a reasoned response. The introduction is particularly impressive with its initial reference to all three sources. The only real criticism would be of the rather assertive conclusion and the failure to use a source in this final statement. This response would secure 9 out of 10 marks.

(b) When Hitler became Chancellor at the beginning of 1933 he was very far from the absolute power he ultimately achieved. First, he had to apply gleichschaltung to the entire Weimar system. There were several obstacles to complete Nazi control. These were groups or institutions which were allowed legal 'organisational space' and hence would have had the ability to offer resistance. These can be broadly summarised into three groups: political groups, civic institutions and the military. The term political groups naturally means the parliamentary ones, but also includes the trade unions due to their political allegiances and agendas and membership systems and the state governments. The civic institutions are the judiciary and the police, the bureaucracies and the civil service. The military covers the army and President Hindenburg, given his military links, and also the SA, despite being of the Nazi group.

Hitler used different tactics to remove the different threats. The use of violence was only part of some solutions. The experience of the Munich Beer Hall Putsch had taught Hitler that the simple use of violence was not suitable to gain power. He also needed legality, or at least the veneer of it.

The first threat to Hitler were the other political parties, not only the left wing, but those which had helped him into power. They could block his changes. He had a majority with the help of the DVP, but not the two-thirds majority necessary for constitutional changes. The important ones to remove first were the pro-democracy left wing. Hitler achieved this through a combination of pseudo-legality, deceit and the use of violence and terror. The first thing Hitler did was to schedule an election for 5 March. This was in the hope of getting a higher percentage of the vote. Playing on the right wing's fear of Marxism and a high vote for the left, Hitler started closing down various liberties and rights, the freedom of the press for example. As Source 4 shows us, another 'pseudo-regularization' took place around this time when several thousand SA members were engaged as 'auxiliary policemen'. The right wing allowed this, as it was targeted against the left wing, 'the SA specialized in attacking first Socialist militants'. The Reichstag fire increased the fear of the right, and led to the Reichstag Fire Decree on 28 February. The Enabling Act removed any vestiges of constitutional power from the left. The necessity for support from the right wing now gone, Hitler then banned their parties as well. The pseudo-legality of the situation wrong-footed the left whilst the violence of the SA closed off other options to them.

The trade unions were similarly deceived and stamped down on. The looming power of the SA made a fight back more difficult, but as Hitler had made the right-wing parties feel more secure with his 'nationalism', he put the trade unions off guard by appearing to pander to the 'socialist' aspect of National Socialism when he made 1 May a national holiday. 2 May brought the ban on trade unions, unexpected and unprepared for.

The permeation of Nazism throughout the civic institutions down to the very lowest levels was highly important and aided in removing the political obstacles. The Nazis wanted to attain complete control. They could not be subject to extra-Nazi standards and controls within the state, but would be above everything. Hence the control of the judiciary and police was key.

Measures leading in this direction were sanctioned by the right-wing parties until their removal and so were closely linked with the removal of the left wing. In February 1933 Goering made the SA auxiliary police part of the plan for the elimination of Marxism. This led to utter lawlessness, although theoretically the judiciary were still in control. The Reichstag Fire Decree allowed for police 'protective custody' without any judicial sentence. From then on what the courts did was irrelevant, as a person could be taken into 'protective custody' at any time, even out of prison. With no cooperation from the police, the courts could not properly challenge any Nazi misdemeanours, and could no longer protect the rights of any defendants, as they could be at any time removed by the Nazis to deal with by themselves. This is what Source 4 emphasises, with the wild camps.

The Enabling Act on 23 March empowered the government to make laws, even laws which deviated from the 1919 Constitution. Hitler became the final authority and could always be relied on to support his men, even if they had been somewhat overzealous.

The sovereignty of the state governments, the individual power bases, was only abolished in January 1934, although the Nazis had long before managed to bypass this, as Source 5, written in April 1933, shows. Again, the Reichstag Fire Decree had allowed for the removal of state governors, in cases where they had lost control. The local SA would cause a commotion, and then complain to the government that the state government had lost control. The state governor would be replaced, usually by the Nazi Gauleiter (area leader).

The Nazi control of the law left their political opponents wrong-footed. They tried to follow the rules, the SPD carefully toeing the line, whilst the Nazis just made them up as they went along. This pretence at legality, manipulation of all the systems allowed the Nazis to stay beyond reproach.

The case of the reactions we can see from the bureaucracies, shows another facet of the power consolidation. However both Sources 5 and 6 emphasise a lack of violence — 'For the moment I am still safe', very different from Source 4. This is because the violence in Source 4 is targeted. There is a bloody week in Kopenick, but Kopenick is one of the 'red' suburbs of Berlin.

Source 5 tells us about the civil service law, which enabled the purge of the civil services of 'undesirables', Jews, those with left-wing loyalties and so forth, and Source 6 supports this, talking of the 'blacklisting of former Socialists from employment possibilities'. One of the ways the Nazis forced consent was by threatening people's jobs. Although many teachers, professors and civil servants lost their jobs, many simply aligned to the new order, even giving up party memberships as early as March 1933. This appears to be just another type of fear, but the line between lack of opposition and consent to the situation becomes very hard to draw. Opportunism grew, many people joining the Nazi Party to advance their positions. There was also popular support. 43.8% of the vote in the elections had been for the Nazis.

Source 5 shows that it is reports of violence, not actually the violence itself, which affected people. The writer's own experience of the Nazis is 'both very polite'. It is the reports he hears which scare him. Source 6 also talks of reports trickling out and scaring people.

It must be remembered though that there was support for the Nazis. Source 6 tells us of a 'roundup of beggars in Northeim'. This was something that was actually very popular. Prior to the Nazis coming to power, people felt unsafe on the streets and were concerned about rising crime levels. Violence directed against social 'unsavouries' was popular. Where people weren't attacked themselves, this being the vast majority, they rationalised and even took advantage of the situation.

Another use of violence which helped the consolidation of power was the use of violence against the SA itself, as depicted in Sources 1, 2 and 3. Hitler turned the violence on his own men. This particular violence, the Night of the Long Knives, had several benefits. As Source 1 shows, it extended Hitler's authority, by removing a potential rival, Röhm. Source 3 shows that it also got rid of the Papen group, another important threat to Hitler, as they were trying to get him removed. Source 2 shows that by acting against both groups simultaneously, Hitler was able to gain gratitude from the army, General Blomberg thanking him for his 'determined and courageous action'. The army were willing to overlook the murder of some of their own men, General Schacht for instance, because, as Source 1 points out, the removal of the SA 'confirmed [the army] in its position as sole arms-bearer'. Germany would not end up with a 'revolutionary people's army' as the generals had feared. Furthermore, the general public were pleased at the removal of the SA, and were happy that Hitler seemed to be becoming more conservative and taking control. It also allowed Hitler to be distanced from the former violence. Something that Source 2 also points out is that despite the popularity of the event, the Nazis were still careful to 'make it legal', with the law they made condoning it in retrospect. Hence Hitler was able to get the army's support purely by careful political manoeuvring. When Hindenburg died, they were happy for him to combine the posts of chancellor and Führer. Hitler was now in supreme control.

To say that violence was the key component of the power consolidation would imply simple and probably completely unworkable methods, but Hitler's were much more complex. He used violence in several ways, simple violence against the left wing (knowing he had the support of the right wing and the majority of the public), subtle hints of violence against the public, and then used violence on the SA, hence putting an end to the overt violence. Legality was an extremely important part of Hitler's strategy, and he out-manoeuvred the majority of his opponents perfectly legitimately. The entire takeover was an incredible piece of PR.

> This response displays many strengths and some weaknesses. The initial impression is that it is overburdened with 'own knowledge' and that the sources are neglected, e.g. there is no source reference in the introduction. However, as the answer progresses, all the sources are used in an intelligent and sensitive way and in mutual support, e.g. Sources 5 and 6 on the rumours of violence and its impact. The strengths outweigh the defects and the answer would be awarded **16 marks** — a clear A grade, although it could perhaps have been achieved with less effort.

■ ■ ■

Answer to question 1: C-grade candidate

(a) The Night of the Long Knives was from 30 June to 2 July 1934. It was a series of arrests and killings by the SS of people who the party needed to get rid of, in order to maintain their power. The main event was the arrest and murder of the SA leaders, including Hitler's once close friend, Ernst Röhm, who had been in the party since the 1923 Putsch. This resulted in the removal of the SA, which was necessary in order to keep Hitler the support of the élite, and therefore in power. Over the three days, many were killed, including Sleicher. Many different people had viable motives for wanting the SA and others removed, and therefore there are many people who were in some way responsible.

Source 1 would suggest that certain individuals within the Nazi Party, i.e. Goering and Himmler, were responsible for the Night of the Long Knives, because they knew that they could gain some personal benefit and power from it. The source details what both men gained after the event and therefore can go some way in explaining why they may have been responsible for making it happen. With the SA and Röhm gone, Himmler could 'develop his SS empire', which in later years gave him immense power within the Nazi regime, i.e. the SS ran the concentration camps. Goering, it states, 'was satisfied with the removal of a rival'. Röhm had been Hitler's 'right-hand man', and his removal made space for Goering to become closer to the Führer, and gain positions, such as being put in charge of the four-year plans in 1936. The source also suggests that Hitler could have been responsible, because he had made a promise to Hindinburg to maintain the army and had kept this promise through carrying out the Night of the Long Knives.

Source 2 strongly suggests that Hitler was responsible for the Night of the Long Knives. Firstly, Hitler actively acknowledges responsibility, by 'stressing that the lightning action had been necessary, otherwise many thousands of people would have been in danger of being wiped out'. Therefore, Hitler does not deny responsibility, but talks about events candidly, suggesting he takes responsibility for it. The source also talks about how Hitler gained great respect and thanks from Blomberg, the head of the army. This was very important, because the Night of the Long Knives was necessary because of the growing problems between the SA and the mainstream army. Therefore, Hitler needed to show support for the army, in order to maintain his power. The response of Blomberg therefore shows that Hitler has been successful in maintaining the support of the army.

Source 3 could be used to suggest that certain individuals, such as Papen and Röhm, were themselves responsible for the Night of the Long Knives, because their actions made it necessary. For example, Röhm was outspoken about wanting a 'second revolution', and this would have scared the élite army. The source talks about him 'conspiring with the French ambassador and Sleicher and Strasser'. It states that Hitler had to take action against these 'rebels', as he needed the élite's support. Papen had also made a speech against the SA and Hitler's support of Röhm therefore could have spurred Hitler on to make the decision to kill Röhm. Therefore Papen or Röhm himself could have been indirectly responsible for the Night of the Long Knives.

> 🅔 This is largely accurate (although there are spelling errors in the names of von Schleicher and Hindenburg) and the question is never forgotten. The chief weakness is the failure to integrate knowledge and sources or to interlink the sources. There is no use of a source in the introductory paragraph and — always a bad sign — the sources are taken in the order they appear. Rather than being used by the writer in the construction of an answer, the sources are allowed to dictate the structure. This answer would be awarded 5 or 6 out of 10 marks.

(b) Even in 1923 terror and violence played an important role in the Nazi policy. When Hitler came into power in 1933 his power was by no means secure and he needed to consolidate this power. Violence was one way that he did this. There were of course many other factors too.

Sources 1, 2 and 3 all talk about the Night of the Long Knives, the most obvious use of violence in the consolidation, and that which probably marked the time when power was consolidated, because afterwards Hindinburg died and Hitler had gained the support of the army, meaning that the two groups who could possibly have taken his power away had been dealt with. This was very important, and violence played an immense role in carrying out the task. Estimates of deaths over the three nights that collectively make up the Night of the Long Knives are variable, although 90 killed is a popular figure. The most famous among the dead were Röhm, who was once Hitler's closest friend, and Sleicher, who had preceded Hitler to the Chancellorship of Germany. Before the Night of the Long Knives, it has been argued that Hitler's power was becoming increasingly compromised because the élite were becoming annoyed with the calling of some, especially Röhm and the SA, for a second revolution. Hitler needed the army onside. He may have also been worried that Röhm was going to try and overthrow him, because he believed that Hitler was not extreme enough in his need to gain complete power. Therefore, the violence used on the Night of the Long Knives was very important in the consolidation of the Nazi regime, because of the outcomes for the party, especially the gain of army support. All three sources mention the fact that Hitler had gained the respect of Blomberg, had got rid of his enemies and was clear in accepting responsibility for the killings. Therefore violence in this case was very important in the power consolidation.

Source 4 talks about how Goering issued the power of auxiliary police to the SA in February 1933. This gave them the power to arrest. Here is another example of the use of violence in the consolidation of power. In order to gain the most power from the SA they were awarded with these extra powers which they could use in the bid to gain a one-party state, and to achieve *Gleichschaltung*. This was a justification for the violent actions of the SA, for example at the Kroll Opera House where they pressurised certain groups into voting Nazi in order to get the two-thirds majority they needed for power. They had also used immense violence in making arrests, removing Communist and socialist enemies and in the aftermath of the Reichstag fire. Therefore, by giving them the police powers the violence was justified. The source talks about how, between them, the SA and the regular police removed and dealt violently with any enemies, therefore showing how important violence was.

However, despite the fact that violence was continually used by the SA and SS in the early power seizure and the striving for *Gleichschaltung* as well as more specifically in high-profile violence such as the Night of the Long Knives, violence was not the only way in which the Nazis consolidated their power. In fact, Hitler strived for legal revolution, even though this meant manipulating the laws. For example, as Source 5 describes, the Civil Service Act was passed to stop any socialists working in the civil service. Although violence was probably used for those who refused to accept the law, the eviction of socialists had been made legal. This was one other way the Nazis had consolidated power, through manipulation of the legal system to bring in laws that legally banned other parties and other people working in the state system.

Source 6 goes on to suggest that although in the early months terror and violence had been 'the most effective means of evoking external compliance', and 'there were still arrests to be made', the consolidation of power, at least in Northeim, was not so violent as made out. It also states that the SA were not really following ordered violence, just doing what they liked, suggesting that violence was not a major planned part of Hitler's consolidation ideas, but more random and spontaneous.

Other techniques were also used. The pseudo legalisation of actions, such as the Enabling Act, the act passed after the Night of the Long Knives, and the Civil Service Act, all made what Hitler was doing legal. This made him appear respectable to the élite. It also justified the violence. Violence was obviously important in coercing the people into doing what the Nazis wanted, and for getting rid of enemies who could damage the regime. The Night of the Long Knives was very important too. I would conclude that violence did play an important role, but so did legal manipulation.

e This exhibits many of the characteristics of the answer to (a). It is largely accurate, it maintains focus and it attempts a debate. However, there is little integration of knowledge with sources or linkage between the sources in either mutual support or contradiction. Important points are missed, e.g. the polite treatment of Klemperer, contrasted with the real threat that he feels. Once again the sources dictate the order of the argument. It would be awarded 10/20 marks.

Question 2

(a) Using your own knowledge and Sources 1, 2 and 5, assess the fear and hostility that the Gestapo inspired within the German public. (10 marks)

(b) Using your own knowledge and all the sources, assess the effectiveness of the Gestapo. (20 marks)

Source 1: *From* The Gestapo is Everywhere, J. De la Rue, 1962

The Gestapo acted on its own account by secretly installing microphones and tape recorders in the homes of suspects. In the absence of the victim, or in the pretext of making repairs or of checking the telephone or the electrical installations, a few microphones were discreetly installed, allowing the individual to be spied upon even in the bosom of his family. No one was safe from this type of practice... Spying became so universal that nobody could feel safe.

Source 2: *From* The Gestapo and German Society, R. Gellately, Clarendon Press, 1991
Cooperation of the German People with the Gestapo in Düsseldorf

The reason the Gestapo began an investigation	Number	Percentage
Reports from the population	213	26
Information from other control organizations	139	17
Observation by Düsseldorf Gestapo agents	127	15
Information from state or local authorities	57	7
Statements at interrogation	110	13
Information from business	24	3
Information from Nazi organization	52	6
No information	103	13
Total	**825**	**100**

Source 3: *From A Message to all Gestapo Officers and to the Political Police of the State. No. 33590 Berlin, 22 April 1936*

Re: Prominent Personalities of the Weimar period [Systemzeit]

A list must be sent in by return of post of those people in your area who were prominent in opposing and slandering the National Socialist movement before the takeover of power. The following details are requested concerning the prominent leaders in politics and business from the camp of the former DNVP, DVP and Democratic

Edexcel Unit 6

Party [*Staatspartei*]: the first name and surname, the date and place of birth, whether or not a Jew, present domicile, profession, including all offices held by the person concerned, whether the person is in receipt of a pension etc. and whether the person had his citizenship revoked or whether an application has been made for the revocation of his citizenship. Furthermore, his present occupation must be reported. At the same time, a detailed report must be made about the incidents in which the individual was involved, particularly hostile activity towards the NSDAP, and whether or not the person in question is still a clandestine opponent.

Source 4: *From* The Nazi Seizure of Power: The Experience of a Single German Town, W. S. Allen, 1965

Hermann Schulze was a rank and file member of the SPD and also of the Reichsbanner. He had worked at the Northeim railroad yards, had lost his job in the purge of 1932, and had furthermore been denied unemployment pay. Hence, he entered the Third Reich fully engrossed with the problem of earning his daily bread. During this period, Schulze and his family lived by working for the peasants around Northeim. He and his children worked all day and received their meals in exchange. His wife was lucky enough to find a job at the cigar factory, and thus they lived. His family was often hungry but his father helped out, sharing what little he had with them. Eventually the peasants refused to give Schulze any more work because they were afraid of what might happen to them if it were discovered that they were helping a Socialist.

During this period the Gestapo searched Schulze's house several times, very carefully. They cut open mattresses and thumped on walls and even broke open a section of the wall that happened to be hollow. They confiscated Schulze's rifle, but Schulze hid the Reichsbanner flag so carefully that they never found it. The Gestapo were very angry about it. They questioned him on that and related matters at least twenty times.

In the summer of 1933, after he had been without work for several months, Schulze was given a job in the stone quarry near Northeim as a result of the intervention of Walter Steineck (who had once courted Schulze's cousin), and in return for a promise to give up political activity. He found many SPD officials from Northeim working there. Every morning they were all made to salute the swastika when it was raised. The work consisted of breaking stones with a sledge hammer and pay was 20 marks a week, which Schulze said was like the old proverb: 'Too much to die on and too little to live on.' It was actually less than the dole.

For Schulze who had worked as track repairman, the work was quite tolerable, but for some it was brutal. Schulze's cousin, who had worked in a bureau in Northeim before the purge of the city employees, died as a result of exposure to the weather. Eventually, in 1935, Schulze found a better job with the Autobahn construction team. During the intervening years the house searches continued. One Gestapo commissar searched Schulze's house at least seven times, and there were others too. 'The worst was hearing the knock on the door and wondering what was going to happen this time.'

He was also watched in other ways. In the winter of 1933–34, an unknown man knocked at Schulze's door and asked for him by name. Schulze took him in. It was raining and the man was wet. The man showed Schulze a Reichsbanner membership book and told him that he was a fugitive from the Gestapo. He told Schulze that the Reichsbanner had risen in the Ruhr and was fighting the Nazis. Would Schulze have any weapons? Could he supply the names of any loyal Reichsbanner men in the area? Schulze answered 'No' to each question and added, 'I'm through, I've had the shit kicked out of me. All I can do is put you up overnight and feed you, which I'd do for any human being on a night like this'.

In the morning, after breakfast, the man went to the door and, just before he left, turned his lapel back and showed Schulze an SS button. Then he left wordlessly.

Source 5: *From* The Nazi Terror, *E. A. Johnson, 1999*

The key to understanding the sometimes brutal, sometimes quasi-legalistic, but always effective Nazi terror lies in its selective nature. Never implemented in a blanket or indiscriminate fashion, it specifically targeted and ruthlessly moved against the Nazi regime's racial, political, and social enemies; at the same time it often ignored or dismissed expressions of non-conformity and mild disobedience on the part of other German citizens. The dualistic treatment of different sections of the German population helped the Nazi regime garner legitimacy and support among the populace. Indeed, many Germans perceived the terror not as a personal threat to them but as something that served their interests by removing threats to their material well-being and to their sense of community and propriety. This acceptance helped guarantee that the leading organs of the terror, like the Gestapo, would not be hampered by limitations to their manpower and means.

Answer to question 2: A-grade candidate

(a) Fear and hostility, though linked, are two separate emotions. The Gestapo did not necessarily inspire both in the German public and nor was it their aim to. The image they attempted to project was intended to instil respect, but they weren't trying to stir up hostility. There has been considerable debate amongst historians over the years on the role and perception of the organisation and the three sources illustrate the evolution of the debate.

In terms of causing fear, the effect they had can be gathered from Source 1. 'Spying became so universal that nobody could feel safe.' The Gestapo image of omnipotence was so successful, whatever its actual strengths, that they became the subject of almost urban myth. Their impact was such that even in 1962 the book analysing them continued to project this image, being called *The Gestapo is Everywhere*. The type of fear generated in the German public, however, can be qualified by referral to Source 5. Because the terror was 'selective', i.e. with a defined target, it was for many Germans not perceived 'as a personal threat'. People knew what rules to follow to stay out of trouble.

The hostility the Gestapo inspired appears, on the other hand, extremely limited. Naturally their victims would dislike them, but rather than hostility, the German public displayed a high level of cooperation. As Source 2 shows, 26% of the leads the Düsseldorf Gestapo received prior to beginning an investigation came from 'reports from the population'. In fact this percentage is extremely low compared to the nationwide average of at least 50%. Moreover these reports appear to have come completely voluntarily, as there is a different category for 'Statements at interrogation'. This high degree of cooperation is further explained by Source 5. The German public felt that the Gestapo 'served their interests'. The explanation Source 5 gives of this benefit talks of the removal of threats to their sense of community and so on, but in fact people used the Gestapo to benefit on a much more direct and personal level. People would denounce unwanted spouses or rich neighbours simply for immediate personal profit.

In conclusion, therefore, the Gestapo inspired general fear, but little hostility. Over time, the terror induced by the Gestapo has been used as an explanation for the continuing control the Nazis achieved over the German public. In that case hostility would be expected. This lack of hostility leads to the conclusion that the effect the Gestapo had on the German public was much more complex. The main part of the reason for the Gestapo's success in producing general fear and appearing omniscient was the way the German public cooperated with the Gestapo. Much more than producing hostility in the people, the Gestapo had the effect of encouraging self-serving opportunism.

> *e* This is a thoughtful and perceptive answer, linking sources and own knowledge and showing an awareness of the historiographical dimension. The candidate would earn 9/10 marks.

(b) The role of the Gestapo was 'to investigate and combat all activity throughout Prussia which poses a threat to the state' as stated in 1936. However, the secret police did eventually cover all German states.

The Gestapo was essentially a repressive organisation, and the image it fostered of itself was that of ruthless effectiveness and all-pervading knowledge. Sources 1 and 4 both support this image. Source 1 portrays the Gestapo as users of insidious modern technology, cunning spies from whom 'nobody could feel safe'. Source 4 develops the unease inspired even further. Their persecution of Schulze, the socialist, was extremely effective, denying him employment. They managed to break his resistance. 'I'm through,' he said. However, it is the twist at the end of the tale which really makes them chilling, the convincing Reichsbanner impostor. The Gestapo is everywhere, it seems.

Sources 3 and 5 support each other, emphasising organisational ability. Source 5 says that the Gestapo 'specifically targeted and ruthlessly moved against the Nazi regime's racial, political and social enemies,' whilst Source 3 expects detailed, exact information 'by return of post'. The Gestapo seems to be living up to its traditional image, an image embodied in the first source and summed up in the title of this 1962 book.

However, the sources do indicate that the Gestapo had weaknesses which could affect their effectiveness. Source 5 talks of the Gestapo having 'limitations to their manpower and means'. In fact Düsseldorf, the area referred to in Source 2, had only 281 agents in 1937, despite being responsible for a population of four million people. That works out as one agent to 14,000 people. This lack of personnel was coupled with another difficulty, demonstrated by Source 3. The majority of the Gestapo's work was bureaucratic. The headquarters demanded long reports and lists. These points now make Source 1 less credible. Would the overworked Gestapo staff really have the time to bug people's homes, let alone listen to all the tapes?

It suddenly seems surprising that the Gestapo managed to build such a reputation. This reputation is partially explained by Source 5, when it says that the Nazi regime managed to garner 'support among the populace.' What this 'support' translates into is shown in Source 2. 'Reports from the population' account for the reason why the Gestapo began an investigation in 26% of the cases in Düsseldorf. Other local case studies have put this percentage as high as even 50% or 80%. This cooperation, though seemingly the ultimate solution, the self-policing population, actually threw up problems of its own.

The Gestapo had to rely on people reporting on each other. Where they didn't, it was often only luck when the Gestapo did stumble across the resistance. Source 4's portrayal of a completely crushed SPD member is not entirely representative. The 'lefties' were undoubtedly repressed, but Germany's socialist party did manage to survive the Third Reich, at least in an 'informal and decentralised form'. In fact Source 4 does hint at this. 'Could he supply the names of any loyal Reichsbanner men in the area?' Not all of them had been tracked down. Also, after about 1943, as people became disillusioned with the Nazis, denunciations dried up, and the Gestapo started having real difficulties.

Another problem with relying on the population was that the population had priorities of its own. Source 5 says that 'it served their interests', referring to their 'sense of community and propriety'. These were not always their reasons, though. Many denunciations stemmed not from political but from personal motivations. People would 'inform' on their unwanted spouses as Communists, hoping the Gestapo would remove them. In other attempts for personal gain, they would denounce neighbours as behaving strangely, hoping to benefit from being able to take over their property. This added to the Gestapo's bureaucratic burden, sifting through the denunciations and trying to decide which ones were genuine. In fact, Himmler was so concerned with this barrage of false, misleading accusations, that he tried to put a halt to it, threatening malicious denouncers with concentration camps themselves. This didn't seem to have too great an effect. The result of this pressure on the Gestapo was that decisions over which cases to pursue had to be made quickly, and tended to be arbitrary, based on the particular officer's priorities. The Gestapo commissar who searched Schultze's house seven times in Source 4 is a good example.

The Gestapo wanted to achieve comprehensive surveillance and perfect repression but because of minimal personnel couldn't achieve this. However, they were still able to produce the image of being extremely powerful, and hence this aspiration had its effects, scaring potential opposition. Within the situation at the time, the Gestapo were effective. Their image may have helped suppress opposition, but it must also be remembered that the Nazi regime was relatively popular, and hence there wasn't very much opposition to suppress. The elusive snippet of the socialist resistance was pretty insignificant anyway. Although there were problems with the cooperation they received from the public, it helped them more than it hindered them.

> This is an excellent response worth 18/20 marks, showing detailed knowledge well integrated with the sources and a sophisticated use of the sources with interlinking and high-level inferential skills, particularly in its use of Source 4. The focus on the question is sharp. Although the historiographical dimension is not fully addressed, it is hinted at and this form of knowledge is not essential.

■ ■ ■

Answer to question 2: C-grade candidate

(a) The Gestapo were the Nazi secret police. They formed part of the SS, although they had been controlled by Goering, not Himmler, until 1936, when Hitler gave Himmler control of all police. It is widely thought that the Gestapo were everywhere, spying on people, arresting, and interrogating, often violently, to gain information on enemies of the regime.

Source 1 would suggest that the Gestapo instilled much fear in the German people. It talks about the techniques they used to spy on people and to gain information. It says that 'spying became so universal that no one could feel safe'. This suggests that people were fearful of the Gestapo, as they didn't feel safe and felt that they could become targets too. The source says that they 'acted on their own account', meaning that they gained all their information themselves through the spying techniques detailed.

A2 History

question 2

Source 2 shows the statistics of 'the cooperation of the German people with the Gestapo in Düsseldorf'. This basically shows the sources from which the Düsseldorf Gestapo gained their information and the percentage of information gained from each source. It shows that 26% of the information came from the German people themselves, presumably meaning that individuals came forward to supply information on others, of their own accord. Therefore this would suggest that there was not much hostility towards the Gestapo, as people were obviously willing to supply information to them. People may have had some fear, which is why they were so willing to supply information. Other statistics show that the percentage of information gained from actual operations by the Gestapo alone, e.g. by interrogation, or from other organisations, is quite low. Therefore, the fact that they relied so strongly on public donations of information suggests there was not much hostility, and also maybe not much fear.

Source 5 suggests that the Gestapo didn't instil much fear or hostility in ordinary German people. It states that people didn't see it as a personal threat but more as 'something that served their interests'. This is because it helped to keep their own lives safe by removing what were seen as 'enemies of the state', i.e. Communists, Jews, etc. Therefore this source would suggest that for the ordinary German, there was not much fear — instead, the Gestapo were seen as protecting their interests. This is because the treatment of people was 'dualistic', they were brutal towards political enemies, but ignored minor 'disobediences' on the part of the ordinary conforming public. Therefore, the source says they gained support, not a fearful and hostile response from the people.

Therefore, different views on the actions of the Gestapo would suggest that the amount of fear and hostility instilled in the German people was variable.

> *e* This has focus and uses the sources sensibly, but it displays very little 'own knowledge' and some of that is incorrect, as Himmler had gained control of the Gestapo in 1934, not 1936, and they were not integrated into the SS until later. It would earn 5/10 marks.

(b) The Gestapo were not formed as part of the SS — they had originally been the Berlin secret police, and hence not all members were Nazi. In 1936 when the control of all police, therefore including the Gestapo, was handed over to Himmler, the role of the Gestapo became even more political than criminal as it was now part of the SS state. However, since 1933, as Source 4 states, the Gestapo were carrying out raids on homes to try to discover political opponents. The role of the Gestapo was to investigate, to arrest any political opposers, such as Jews, Communists and socialists. However, it is questionable how effective they actually were in regard to carrying out these tasks.

Source 1 would suggest that the Gestapo were very effective, as 'nobody could feel safe'. This must suggest that their techniques were so effective that they managed to scare everyone and make their presence shown to everyone. The techniques of using secretly installed microphones to spy on people, which were installed 'in the pretext of...checking the telephone line or electrical installations', also show how effective they were, as they used clever, devious tricks in order to carry out these investigations. Therefore, Source 1 would suggest that the Gestapo were quite effective, especially in convincing people that they needed to be on their guard.

Source 2 suggests that in some ways the Gestapo were not effective. They obviously relied heavily on public support, with information volunteered by the public forming 26% of the reasons behind cases being investigated. Only 15% of the information leading to an investigation was from observations of Gestapo officers. This therefore suggests that they weren't effective because they relied so heavily on other people and groups for information — without public support a quarter of the cases investigated would have gone unknown. Also most of the other cases came from information from non-Gestapo, i.e. business. The fact that 13% of cases were investigated on no information suggests they were random, and just made lucky guesses as to who should be investigated, therefore showing them to be ineffective in finding their own intelligence information. It is true, however, that the Gestapo were not very numerous, especially in street presence, so therefore it may have been more difficult to keep track themselves of everything that was happening.

Source 3 shows that the Gestapo are well organised, because they have all this information that has been requested by the head of the police, about the enemies of the regime, i.e. Communists and Jews. This shows they must be effective because the fact that the information is needed by return of post would suggest that they already have the information and therefore are effective because they keep up to date with what is going on. Therefore, this source would suggest that the Gestapo were very effective, because they have so much complex information to hand.

Source 4, in my opinion, shows that the Gestapo were in some ways quite effective, but also not. The fact that they realised that this man was an 'enemy of the regime', i.e. he was a member of the SPD and the Reichsbanner, suggests that they did know what was happening around them and who were the opponents that needed to be sorted out. They were also thorough in their techniques — they had pinpointed Schulze as an opponent and then used several techniques to try to prove it in order to remove him. They searched his house several times and also used a clever trick, by sending the SS man in dressed as a Gestapo fugitive, to try to trick him into admitting membership of the Reichsbanner. Therefore we might think from this that the Gestapo were effective and thorough in who they investigated. However, the fact that after so much hard work they still could not prove that he was a member of the SPD and the Reichsbanner suggests they may be not so effective. The amount of times they searched the house and found nothing, even though Schulze had a Reichsbanner flag, suggests that the efficiency may not be as clear as it appears. He did not even fall for the con trick. Therefore, although the Gestapo were efficient in pinpointing who they wanted, they were not efficient at actually incriminating them.

question 2

Source 5 would suggest the Gestapo were limited by 'manpower and means', which could have led to their inefficiency. It talks about public support for them, but the fact that a secret police group were seen as protectors of personal material goods may suggest that they were not so effective in doing what they were meant to be doing, arresting and removing opponents of the Nazi regime. If the majority of people were not scared of their power, this could suggest they were not very efficient in carrying out their tasks.

The question of Gestapo effectiveness is obviously unanswerable, if these sources are anything to go by. They all appear to give conflicting arguments. Some would suggest that they were effective and some would suggest that they were incredibly ineffective. I think that they were ineffective, because of the statistics in Source 2 and the fact they had very limited means and funds for carrying out the investigations. There were many other control groups such as the SD and the mainstream SS themselves who also carried out arrests and interrogations, and therefore the Gestapo alone were hampered by problems, meaning they had to rely on public information, not their own investigative evidence.

> This does attempt to maintain focus on the question in a very simple and straightforward way. There is an appreciation that a source can be ambivalent and be used to support both sides of the argument. There are, however, serious weaknesses. Once again there is very little 'own knowledge' and what there is, is not very reliable, i.e. the final comment on the SS. There is no attempt to interlink the sources, e.g. to use Source 4 to illustrate the conclusions in Source 5. There is some confusion about the meaning of 'effective' in the use of Source 2. Just because they relied on public cooperation does not mean that they were ineffective, possibly just the opposite. Finally, there is no attempt to set the sources in a context of historiographical knowledge. The response would be awarded 10/20 marks.

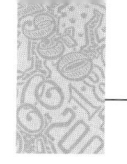

Question 3

(a) Using your own knowledge and Sources 1, 2 and 3, explain how Goebbels and the Nazi regime sought to control and use the media to their advantage. (10 marks)

(b) Using your own knowledge and all the sources, assess the effectiveness of Nazi propaganda. (20 marks)

Source 1: *From* A Social History of the Third Reich, *R. Grunberger, 1971*

The linchpin of its whole apparatus of regimentation and pre-censorship were what were called language rulings; these were directives issued in the course of daily briefings at the Propaganda Ministry and transmitted to all editorial desks in the country. As soon as the editors concerned had assimilated their instructions they were duty bound to destroy every trace of them and sign affidavits to that effect. The directives themselves were so minutely detailed and so destroyed all journalistic initiative that Goebbels, in a moment of candour, admitted, 'Any person with the slightest spark of honour left in him will take good care in future not to become a journalist.' Quite a few practising journalists, actually, far from resenting the fact that their columns had become official notice-boards, welcomed Goebbels' scheme because it freed them from the burden of responsibility.

The Press directives were staggeringly comprehensive; head-lines like COMMANDER-IN-CHIEF OF THE NAVY RECEIVES THE FÜHRER were declared inadmissible, for the reason that a subordinate could not receive his supreme commander. Thomas Mann was never to be mentioned, even critically, because his name was to be expunged from the consciousness of all Germans. Charlie Chaplin was to be treated in the same way. Greta Garbo, on the contrary, had to be handled in a friendly manner. Even more positive — in fact, *sympathisch* — was the obligatory press reaction to the Duke of Windsor's wedding. There were to be no press photographs showing cabinet ministers attending banquets, nor any reports on them. Other censored news included outbreaks of cattle-poisoning resulting from the effect of German potassium on cattle fodder, and a car accident involving von Ribbentrop.

Source 2: *From* Nazi Germany, *Klaus P. Fischer, 1995*

The Nazis also made extensive use of film because they recognized, in Goebbels's words, that film was one of the most influential means of reaching a mass audience. In July 1933, Goebbels set up a new film office and later incorporated it into a branch of the Reich Cultural Chamber. As head of his own film credit bank, he advanced considerable sums of money to filmmakers who spoke the language of National Socialism. In addition, the government coordinated the four major film studios — UFA, Bavaria, Terra, and Tobis — by bringing them under the control of a new government-controlled UFA, headed by Fritz Hippler.

During the Third Reich, 1,363 feature films were made. These fell into two broad categories: propaganda and entertainment pictures. Generally all of them were accompanied by the *Deutsche Wochenshau* (German weekly newsreel), which was the only visual source of information the Germans received of the outside world. The majority of the films were simple entertainment that served escapist purposes. Goebbels strongly believed that too much propaganda, especially bad propaganda, was counterproductive. This is why he allowed directors, script writers, and actors considerable freedom to produce their own films as long as they stayed away from political topics. The result, however, was bland uniformity. Most entertainment films presented a sanitized image of carefree life under the protective umbrella of the Nazi regime.

Source 3: *From a speech by Goebbels to senior radio executives, March 1933*

We make no bones about the fact that the radio belongs to us and to no one else. And we will place the radio in the service of our ideology [*Idee*] and [the speaker bangs on the lectern] no other ideology will find expression here... The radio must subordinate itself to the goals which the Government of the national revolution has set itself. The Government will give the necessary instructions...

I consider radio to be the most modern and most crucial instrument that exists for influencing the masses. I also believe — one should say that out loud — that radio will in the end replace the press...

First principle: At all costs avoid being boring. I put that before *everything*... So do not think that you have the task of creating the correct attitudes, of indulging in patriotism, of blasting out military music and declaiming patriotic verse — no, that is not what the new orientation is all about. Rather you must help to bring forth a nationalist art and culture which is truly appropriate to the pace of modern life and to the mood of our times. The correct attitudes must be conveyed but that does not mean they must be boring. And simply because you have the task of taking part in this national enterprise you do not have *carte blanche* to be boring. You must use your imagination, an imagination which is based on sure foundations and which employs all means and methods to bring to the ears of the masses the new attitude in a way which is modern, up to date, interesting, and appealing; interesting, instructive, but not schoolmasterish. Radio must never go down with the proverbial disease — the intention is clear and it puts you off.

Source 4: *From* The Nazi Seizure of Power: The Experience of a Single German Town, *W. S. Allen, 1965*

But already by 1934 enthusiasm for mass demonstrations had fallen off to the point where Northeimers made themselves conspicuous at the beginning of celebrations and then ducked down side streets to avoid having to listen to the speeches. Advertisements for Nazi-sponsored events made increasing use of absolute imperatives such as: 'The *entire* population of Northeim *must* appear!'

The apathy even pervaded the ranks of the NSDAP, and members were required to bring 'control-cards' to meetings to be punched. Anyone who missed three meetings was threatened with expulsion. Members of the NSDAP were also required to bring others with them to meetings so that the halls would be filled. In a memorandum circulated in the summer of 1935 this concept is repeated several times:

> *Every member must look upon it as their duty to attend and to bring several other Volk-comrades with him... Every party-comrade and comrades has the duty of making extensive propaganda for attendance at this meeting so that the very last of all citizens attends... No citizen must be allowed to stay at home...*

Despite these measures and despite the terror that was there to enforce compliance, the history of mass propaganda in the mature dictatorial structure in Northeim was one of increasing indifference. More and more Northeimers were bored and exhausted by Nazi dynamism and complained about the incessant meetings, parades, and demonstrations.

Source 5: *From* The Past is Myself, *Christabel Bielenberg, an opponent of the Nazi regime*

The newspapers and also the wireless, controlled by Dr Goebbels and his Ministry of Propaganda and Public Enlightenment, had become a remorseless hammer-beat of superlatives which, for me at least, successfully defeated their own ends. No one person could be so perfect as the Führer, no race so heroic, so long suffering as the German, so idiotic as the British, or so diabolical as the Jewish — I simply gave up.

Peter relied for information on his efforts to read between the lines of the *Frankfurter Allgemeine Zeitung*. It was to me a rather turgid sheet, but one which had the reputation of having developed quite a technique in camouflaged reporting. I began a serious study of the London *Times*, believing sincerely, as I had been brought up to do, that it would convey to me a balanced and objective viewpoint. It seemed that others had been brought up to think likewise, as *The Times* was not always easy to come by in Hamburg. It was sold out unless I arrived at the newspaper kiosk on time.

(This extract from *The Past is Myself*, first published by Chatto and Windus Ltd, 1968, now published by Corgi, © Christabel Bielenberg, is reproduced by kind permission of the author.)

question 3

Answer to question 3: A-grade candidate

(a) It is obvious from the three sources that the media played a very important role in the consolidation of Nazi power, and that Joseph Goebbels, as Minister for Propaganda, was instrumental in exploiting this to its full potential. Nazi propaganda took many forms; rallies and parades portrayed a feeling of inclusion, or belonging to something highly powerful and important, while grandiose architecture and art attacked the modern and decadent and again portrayed immense physical power. The use of the media fits into the idea of *Gleichschaltung*, the bringing together or coordination of everything into Nazism, and the rejection and removal of any non-Nazi factions. All types of media were manipulated cleverly to show to the German nation the power of its leader and government, and how effective the Nazi regime was. The media provided a means of getting the message to every German.

As Source 1 states, the written media, i.e. newspapers and magazines, were strongly regulated by Nazi directives, which controlled what was reported on and how journalists wrote. The source states that 'the directives themselves were so minutely detailed...and so destroyed all journalistic initiative'. This shows how the Nazis used their control to limit what appeared in the written press to items that would benefit them. This was an effective tool in limiting the influence of other opposition groups or anti-Nazi ideas. For example, as the source states, 'Thomas Mann was never to be mentioned, even critically...because his name was to be expunged from the consciousness of all Germans'. This shows how limited the written media were — the directives which Goebbels had issued were so comprehensive that newspapers were powerless except to publish material deemed suitable by the government. However, the Nazis never controlled every company, unlike with the other media, such as films, where Source 2 talks about the coordination of the film companies under Nazi rule. In Germany at the time there were over 1,000 publications, and most remained privately owned. This could be linked to the comment from Goebbels, that 'any person with the slightest spark of honour left in them will take good care in future not to become a journalist'. This suggests that he believes that written media are 'finished' and will be overtaken by other media.

As Source 2 states, film and television were new phenomena that Goebbels employed in order to take the Nazi message to the people. Goebbels himself was obsessed with film and regularly spent hours watching the latest big screen releases. He had clear ideas about what he liked and what he didn't, and this was portrayed in how he organised the films that were produced and shown in Germany during the Nazi period. As Source 2 states, he set up a new film office in 1933, which along with his own film credit bank, he used to employ the services of film makers who were willing to portray Nazi ideology in their films. Goebbels' main idea for propaganda, as Source 3 states, was that it should be entertaining, 'at all costs avoid being boring'. This is reflected in the film industry: 'the majority of the films were simple entertainment that served escapist purposes'. He believed that if the films were entertaining, people would enjoy them and therefore see Nazism in a similar way instead of as a dull and boring movement. Many of the films were fictional stories, which carried below the plot Nazi ideology such as anti-Semitism, or anti-socialism. They also showed characters who were 'real' Germans, i.e. Aryans.

The other type of film, as the source states, was 'propaganda'. These films were grandiose in scale and portrayed the view of the strong party with its wide-ranging influence and powerful leader. *Triumph of the Will,* by Leni Riefenstahl, chronicled the 1936 Nuremberg rallies. The long shots of rows of marching soldiers and workers, united under the banner of the swastika, and symbolic representations of the Führer as a godlike figure, created this type of effect. Goebbels, however, despised this film, preferring more entertaining films with a message. However, such propaganda showed the immense power of Nazism in a graphic and physical way.

The Nazi film industry was cosmopolitan, they created a big star system, taking 'suitable' (Aryan) actresses and turning them into big screen superstars. There was an emphasis on glamour and a 'Hollywood' style. This would seem strange, as Source 1 shows how the written press was banned from talking about Charlie Chaplin. However, it seems that through the German film industry and such stars as Greta Garbo, Goebbels was trying to show that Nazism could equal and beat whatever America could do. For Goebbels, the cinema was an important way of getting the message to the masses. They even took travelling cinemas to the villages in order to show these films to the people. Similarly, as the source states, the films were accompanied by the *Deutsche Wochenschau*, which was the German newsreel, which was again used to show Nazism in a positive light and emphasise its ideals. It seems that the cinema was about creating the *Volksgemeinschaft*, the people's community, bringing everyone together under one banner.

Source 3 discusses the use of radio as an item of propaganda. Goebbels obviously viewed radio as the main means of getting his message to the German people: 'I also believe...that radio will replace the written press', 'I consider radio to be the most modern and most crucial instrument that exists for influencing the masses.' This links to the comments about the written press in Source 1, and suggests that the radio may be the replacement medium for the written press. Therefore we can see a link between the two sources regarding the opinions of Goebbels as to which medium is best for propaganda. As with film, as mentioned in Source 2, he saw the most important role of the radio as being entertainment, with a message hidden. Radio was an important tool because it was cheap. Goebbels had cheap radio sets mass produced, so that there could be one in every home. He also produced them so that they could only be tuned into Nazi stations, which meant that they could only listen to propaganda. However, as well as having a radio in every home, Goebbels was a fan of communal listening, where, much in the same way as cinema, people would congregate to listen to broadcasts together, in order to discuss together what was being said. This again was a part of *Gleichschaltung*, the bringing together of people under the Nazi ideals. It helped spread the word and increase the feeling of unity of the Nazi movement. Radio was used to broadcast speeches from Hitler, Goebbels and other party leaders and newsreels,

A2 History

question 3

as well as entertainment, which played the same role as film did. As Source 2 states, it 'presented a sanitised image of a carefree life under the protective umbrella of the Nazi regime'.

Therefore we can see that the media played a very important role in Nazi propaganda. Goebbels used his influence to limit and control the media, to make sure that what was written or broadcast was pro-Nazi, portrayed Nazi ideals and extended the idea of integration and coordination of everything under the umbrella of the regime. For those involved in the media, as Source 1 states, the period was creatively limiting, as it was obligatory to follow the strict rules imposed by the propaganda ministry. The film industry boomed in the period, as the source states: '1,363 feature films were made' and many actresses became famous stars and torch bearers for the regime. However, for some, like Leni Riefenstahl, involvement in propaganda films marred the lives of those involved. Goebbels was passionate about film and radio and used his propaganda genius to cleverly exploit them to the benefit of the party. Everyone was involved in the propaganda because it was everywhere. The media allowed the Nazi message to be broadcast to all Germans, everywhere in Germany. It seems that the promotion of the *Volksgemeinschaft* is the main aim of the propaganda. The cinema is obviously a communal activity, and the radio could be made so. However, reading newspapers is obviously an individual act. Therefore, this could suggest why Goebbels does not like the written press, because it cannot bring the people together in the people's community, to watch, listen and then more importantly discuss and believe the propaganda.

> This shows an excellent display of knowledge combined with source use. For a 10-mark question, there is possibly too much. Although the sources tend to be used in the order presented, this might be considered perfectly legitimate in the context of this question. They are interwoven and the sources do not dictate the shape and structuring of the argument, but are used intelligently.

(b) Dr Goebbels' propaganda machine is one of the things which Nazi Germany was most infamous for. Goebbels' techniques are said to have been incredibly advanced, decades ahead of the rest of the world. Nazi propaganda should have been effective. However, both Sources 4 and 5 show the system as not working on the public. According to Source 5, neither the newspapers nor the radio were convincing, 'a remorseless hammerbeat of superlatives...successfully defeated their own ends'. Source 1 shows this attitude towards the newspapers as understandable. They were so completely censored that Goebbels said 'any person with the slightest spark of honour left in him will take good care in future not to become a journalist.' Goebbels did not consider the newspapers a good medium for propaganda — he was more interested in other areas. In Source 3 he says, 'I also believe...that radio will in the end replace the press.'

Unfortunately, even in simply censoring the papers, Goebbels seems to have failed. Source 5 tells us of the 'camouflaged reporting' one newspaper had developed

Edexcel Unit 6

and which it had a 'reputation' for. Also the author of Source 5, Christabel Bielenberg, read instead *The Times*, the British newspaper, which was so popular it was often 'sold out'. People often found ways of getting around the censorship.

Bielenberg's criticism of the radio is much more damning. Not only did Goebbels take it very seriously as a tool for propaganda, the 'most crucial instrument that exists for influencing the masses', but he also told radio executives: 'At all costs avoid being boring. I put that before everything....' He again seems to have failed.

Source 4 appears to expand what Source 5 is saying, but to a much wider group, the villagers of Northeim, and to a different form of propaganda, the mass demonstrations which people were supposed to participate in. It says that the people were 'bored and exhausted' and 'complained about the incessant meetings, parades, and demonstrations.'

In the light of these two sources, Goebbels' propaganda machine appears to have been ineffective. However, are these two sources really suitable representatives of the reaction to propaganda? The audience for propaganda stressed in both Source 2 and 3 is 'the masses'. Hitler said that the consumers of propaganda were the 'less educated masses', and that propaganda was to be addressed 'always and exclusively to the masses'. The 'scientifically trained intelligentsia' were not so easily convinced, and, as a minority, much less important. Returning to Source 5, Christabel Bielenberg does appear to be one of these intelligentsia. She has been 'brought up' to believe that the London *Times* has a 'balanced and objective viewpoint.' Not many parents would have taught their children this. Moreover, she is sufficiently competent in English, a foreign language, to read a newspaper in it. She is obviously highly educated, from a highly educated background. Peter, who 'reads between the lines', also displays a degree of analytical skill not common to the mass of people at that time. These methods of gathering information would not have been available to the majority of German people. The 'reputation' the paper which did 'camouflaged reporting' built up was probably within a circle of friends only, and the 'sold out' *Times* can easily have sold out to this highly educated minority, doubtless not having too high a circulation in Germany anyway. The source does not specify the date when Bielenberg was able to buy *The Times* in Germany. Considering the Nazi control, it would probably have been banned if it were too critical. (Funnily enough, even access to *The Times* may not have been that helpful. Bielenberg's comment about believing it to have a 'balanced and objective viewpoint' is made in a somewhat ironic tone. Before the war, Hitler and his regime were quite popular with the British press.) Bielenberg's reaction to the propaganda is only representative of this intellectual minority, and the oppositional part of it at that, not the mass of the German people.

Once Source 4 is no longer being linked with Source 5 it gives a different interpretation. The apathy with the demonstrations is understandable. They do seem incessant. This had been something the Nazis misjudged. However, the source tells us that there had originally been 'enthusiasm' for these mass demonstrations. The Northeimers might have lost the energy to be actively involved, but they could passively absorb the propaganda in other ways.

In fact, the less demanding Nazi propaganda has been shown to be efficient. The fall in the readership of newspapers may seem to prove otherwise, but Goebbels was actually trying to stifle this activity, judging it too individual and allowing for non-conformity. From Sources 3 and 2, the Nazi emphasis on the radio and film is evident. They are both government coordinated and owned: 'The radio belongs to us and no one else.'

The radio appears to have been relatively successful on 'the masses'. The Nazis ensured that everyone had access, firstly through selling very cheap 'people's receivers' — *Volksempfänger* — and secondly through setting up loudspeakers in public areas such as town squares, where everyone would be required to listen communally. Even with the *Volksempfänger*, where listening could be less communal, the propaganda seems to have been effective. The Nazis distributed large quantities of these radios within Austria, prior to the referendum over the Anschluss there in 1938, and it is believed that it was the convincing effect of the Nazi propaganda coming from these things which led to the 90% 'yes' vote.

Goebbels' attitude towards films also appears to have been effective. Source 2 says that he believed that 'too much propaganda, especially bad propaganda, was counterproductive'. Films were to entertain primarily, with subtle propaganda messages woven in. The Nazis' own market research showed that this approach was effective. People enjoyed the films and understood the messages. For example, after a screening of *Jud Süss*, an anti-Semitic 'historical' drama, a band of Hitler Youth actually murdered a Jewish man. The effects were not always as violent as this, but the films did manage to foster and develop the attitudes and cooperation the Nazis wanted.

In conclusion, Nazi propaganda was highly effective. Naturally it didn't work on everyone, but it wasn't meant to. Goebbels understood that there was little propaganda could do in terms of the opposition intellectuals except to keep their views out of the media and scare them from direct opposition. He couldn't convince them. Not all Nazi propaganda worked on the masses either. The type which demanded active involvement, such as demonstrations, was not always popular. However, the more subtle propaganda, which people could absorb passively, was effective. It must be remembered, though, that propaganda could not really change attitudes, only develop and strengthen them. As Hitler said, the propagandist is there to 'canalise an already existing stream'. The propaganda was effective in Nazi Germany because a large proportion had voted for and supported the Nazis.

> The opening paragraph indicates an A-grade answer with its focus, use of four sources and the interlinking of these sources. This standard is maintained throughout with perceptive source analysis, including inferential skills and use of

the source attributions to make a judgement on utility. The knowledge is extensive and intelligently deployed with information from the sources. This candidate would earn 19/20 marks.

■ ■ ■

Answer to question 3: C-grade candidate

(a) Propaganda played a very important role in the Nazi regime. The propaganda was split into two broad types: firstly there were the parades, uniforms and symbols, which gave a feeling of belonging. Secondly was media propaganda, the use of the mass media to get the Nazi message across to the German people. Joseph Goebbels was head of the propaganda ministry and cleverly used the media to get the ideological message of Nazism across.

Source 1 talks about how the Nazis sought to control the written press. It explains several directives, which Goebbels made to the newspapers, which dictated what could and could not be published in the German newspapers. For example, certain people were not to be mentioned, such as Thomas Mann and Charlie Chaplin. The extract says that the directives were so comprehensive that they 'destroyed all journalistic initiative'. This shows how the regime was controlling the media, to make sure that there were no damaging stories or information relayed to the German people.

Source 2 talks about the use of film as propaganda. Goebbels was a film fanatic, and spent much money on the German film industry. This could explain why so many films were made during the period. The idea of cinema was to bring people together in a collective group, to experience the propaganda together. There were two types of film, entertainment and propaganda. Goebbels, as the source states, believed that entertainment was better than long, informative and instructional films, and therefore most films were stories with underlying Nazi messages. Therefore, cinema was used to portray 'a sanitized image of carefree life under the protective umbrella of the Nazi regime', instead of instructional propaganda.

Source 3 talks about the use of radio. As Goebbels states, 'I consider radio to be the most modern and most crucial instrument that exists for influencing the masses'. He obviously sees the radio as being vitally important as a means for portraying the Nazi message to the people. Radios were cheap to produce, and the party commissioned the production of radios cheap enough so that every German home could have one. They also created radios that could only be tuned into Nazi stations. This shows how they controlled the media to make sure that everyone got to hear their message.

Therefore, here we see three examples of how the Nazis used the different mass media to broadcast the Nazi message, and how they controlled the media so that they only broadcast what the Nazis wanted the people to know about.

question

🅔 Once again this exhibits a common failure to interlink the sources and a tendency to let them dictate the structure of the essay. Some 'own knowledge' is provided in the introduction and the section on radio, and this knowledge is accurate and relevant. It would be worth 5/10 marks.

(b) Propaganda played an immensely important role throughout the Nazi regime, from the consolidating of power in 1933–34 to preparing the German people for war in the summer of 1939. Propaganda took several forms, which fell broadly into two categories. Firstly, there was propaganda which was meant to portray a sense of belonging to something big (the party), unity, power and order. There were parades, huge rallies, architecture, flags and symbols and uniforms. Secondly there was media propaganda, which was intended to spread the message of Nazism and Nazi ideology across Germany, and later the occupied territories. This took the form of newspapers, films and radio broadcasts. Joseph Goebbels, often referred to as the poison dwarf, was the mastermind of the whole operation, in his position as Minister for Propaganda and Popular Enlightenment. He was a propaganda genius, without whom the party may not have been successful in portraying their message to the world.

Source 1 talks about the use of the written media as propaganda. The fact that the newspapers were so controlled by the directives which Goebbels had issued, to govern everything that could be and could not be published, would suggest that the newspapers must have been very effective in portraying the message. Anyone who read a newspaper would have read only what the party wanted them to read. For example, as the source states, 'there were to be no press photographs showing cabinet ministers attending banquets, nor any reports on them'. Here we can see how the party could control exactly what they wanted people to see and read, and also what they didn't want people to know about. Therefore, Source 1 would suggest that the newspaper propaganda was effective because it was so effectively controlled.

Source 2 goes on to talk about the use of film, a particular fascination of Goebbels. This could account for the reason that so many films were made in that time. For Goebbels, film was incredibly important because cinema was transportable, and provided a collective experience, therefore reinforcing the idea of *Gleichschaltung*, togetherness. The films were mainly entertainment because Goebbels didn't want to bore his audience, so they usually had a hidden Nazi message. This was instead of obvious propaganda showing the party strength through rallies, etc. Goebbels believed that entertainment was the key. The films were quite popular and therefore cinema was effective propaganda. It also created big stars and a Hollywood-style industry, showing strength. Everyone could gain the Nazi message from a collective enjoyable experience, so in this respect propaganda was effective.

Source 3 is about radio, another thing Goebbels liked because it brought everyone together collectively but also allowed everyone to listen because it was so cheap. He believed that it would take over from other forms of propaganda because it was so accessible to so many people. They created cheap radios that could only receive Nazi-approved stations, therefore everyone was forced to listen to broadcasts that were intended to entertain and inform the masses on the Nazi viewpoint. Radio was so accessible it was an extremely important and effective form of propaganda.

Source 4 talks about the other sort of propaganda and suggests that it was maybe not as effective as media propaganda. It talks about Northeim and how everyone was fed up with being forced to go to the endless demonstrations and parades. Even party members didn't want to go, and effectively had to 'sign in' to prove they had attended all the rallies. It also talks about the fact that people made themselves seen early on so that they could disappear after the rally had started, just to avoid it. Also, the memorandum of 1935, which basically said it was a German's duty to attend the Nazi demonstrations, was quite ineffective as people were constantly complaining about the endless parades they had to endure. Therefore, this would suggest that at least in some places, especially as the regime had become more established, people were indifferent to the propaganda. Therefore, it cannot have been that effective, with people only going along because they were forced to, not because they wanted to. Therefore they probably didn't take in much of the events as they were so repetitive. Therefore, not all propaganda was so effective.

Source 5 talks about the need of the people to buy newspapers from other places to avoid Nazi propaganda, even to the point that stalls had sold out of London papers. Therefore people didn't read the newspapers they were meant to, and were obviously bored by the propaganda, suggesting it wasn't so effective.

Propaganda was an important tool for the party. I think it was very effective, and especially in the early years — if Goebbels hadn't been in charge, the position of the party could have been different. However, other factors were important, too, in maintaining the party position. However, propaganda on the whole was effective, even though people did get bored with it. The fact that Goebbels identified the need to entertain, instead of just continually inform and instruct, paved the way to the effectiveness of the Nazi propaganda, even though, as with everything, people got bored with it.

> *e* This has limited 'own knowledge' and again a failure to link the sources. Source 1 could be linked to 5 on the dreariness of the press under the Nazis. The sources are understood and perfectly valid conclusions are drawn, but they are used discretely and are allowed to dictate the structure. There is no attempt to use the attribution in Source 5, which might call into question its utility. With Source 4 there is a hint of awareness of this with the phrase 'at least in some places', picking up on the reference to a single German town in the attribution. The candidate would be awarded 10/20 marks.

Question 4

(a) **Using your own knowledge and Sources 1, 2 and 4, explain to what extent and why Goering had been able to build up such a position of power in the Third Reich.** (10 marks)

(b) **Using your own knowledge and all the sources, assess to what extent the political system of the Third Reich was marked by a constant struggle for power and influence among Hitler's subordinates.** (20 marks)

Source 1: *From* Stalin and Hitler, A. Bullock, 1991

The second example, the Four-Year Plan, provided a personal power base for Goering. His original position as Minister-President and Minister of the Interior in Prussia had been eroded by the amalgamation of the Reich and Prussian Ministries of the Interior under Frick, and by the monopoly of control over the police being built up by Himmler and Heydrich. The one real asset he preserved from the Prussian episode was his personal intelligence and research agency, the *Forschungsamt*, based on telephone-tapping and monitoring radio and telegraph communications, which gave him an important advantage over rival Nazi bosses. But he failed to secure the leading place he hoped for in foreign policy and military affairs, and he held no party office which would enable him to compete with Himmler, Goebbels, and Ley, all three of whom combined power in the party with governmental office.

Goering rebuilt his position by extending the scope of the Reich Aviation Ministry which Hitler had set up as a Supreme Reich Authority under his direction in May 1933. He defeated the attempt of the army and Ministry of Defence to keep the new Luftwaffe and its massive armaments programme under their control, and used the latter to break through into the economic field, not only capturing the leading position in it, but re-establishing himself in Hitler's confidence to the point where he was seen as the Führer's second in command.

Source 2: *From* Decree on the Execution of the Four-Year Plan, 18 October 1936

The realization of the new Four-Year Plan as proclaimed by me at the Party Congress of Honour [*Parteitag der Ehre*] requires the uniform direction of all the powers of the German nation and the rigid consolidation of all the pertinent authorities within Party and State.

I assign the execution of the Four-Year Plan to Minister-President General Goering.

Minister-President General Goering will take the necessary measures for the fulfilment of the task given him, and in this respect he has authority to issue legal decrees and general administrative regulations. He is authorized to hear and to issue instructions to all authorities, including the Supreme Authorities of the Reich, and all agencies of the Party, its formations and affiliated organizations.

ADOLF HITLER

Source 3: *From* Inside the Third Reich, A. Speer, 1970

I often asked myself whether Hitler was open to influence. He surely could be swayed by those who knew how to manage him. Hitler was mistrustful, to be sure. But he was so in a cruder sense, it often seemed to me; for he did not see through clever chess moves or subtle manipulation of his opinions. He had apparently no sense for methodical deceit. Among the masters of that art were Goering, Goebbels, Bormann, and, within limits, Himmler. Since those who spoke out in candid terms on the important questions usually could not make Hitler change his mind, the cunning men naturally gained more and more power.

Source 4: *From* Goering, R. J. Overy, 1984

Goering enjoyed, too, the advantage of widespread personal popularity, which was true of none of the conservatives. His exposure to the German public was carefully cultivated. He posed during 1936 and 1937 as the champion of national solutions against the corrupt self-interest of the old elites and big business. The press was largely on Goering's side. Goebbels' propaganda machine heralded the new direction in economic life. Under such circumstances there was no question of dislodging Goering. There were certainly other Nazi claimants, but they were either too weak to oppose Goering, as was Keppler, or too involved in jurisdictional battles of their own, as was Ley. Goering rode roughshod over them all, supported by an ever-growing circle of subordinate officials who could see which way the wind was blowing and hurried to identify their cause with his.

Among the Nazi leadership he was increasingly isolated and distant, able, as long as he enjoyed Hitler's support, to ignore many of the squabbles that went on around him. Other Nazi leaders were envious of his popularity and of his political revival after the disasters of 1933 and 1934. Hess became so obsessively jealous that he tried to suppress newspaper pictures of Goering that flattered his figure. Rosenberg hated him for his threats to uncover what he had been doing in Russia between 1917 and 1919. Julius Streicher published allegations that Goering's first child, Edda, born in 1938, had been artificially inseminated (though it cost him his post as Gauleiter of Nuremberg). More scurrilous still it was rumoured that Mussolini was the father. Ribbentrop, who was jealous of Goering's popularity and social ease abroad, called him in public 'that Christmas tree', a reference to his bemedalled appearance. Himmler and Goebbels tolerated him because he posed no threat to them, nor they to him.

Nor did Goering spare his colleagues, for whom he had scant respect or liking. Keitel and Lammers he hated — 'mere secretaries' — for worming their way between himself and Hitler. Ribbentrop he nicknamed 'Germany's no. 1 parrot' for repeating whatever Hitler said. Only Heydrich, Himmler's deputy, impressed him. Later in the war he said that Heydrich had been 'one of the only real men in Germany'. He had certainly been one of the few men able to play Goering at his own political game.

Source 5: *From* Goering, *R. Manvell and H. Fraenkel, 1962*

It is impossible now to determine the exact degree to which Goering was directly involved in planning the downfall of Blomberg and Fritsch. That he was ready to take advantage of any circumstances that might arise to remove them seems to be certain. His chief accuser remains Gisevius, who claimed at the Nuremberg Trial that it was Goering who encouraged the Field-Marshal's marriage to a woman he already knew to be disreputable in order to make his position untenable, and that in the case of Fritsch it was Goering himself who threatened Schmidt with death at a meeting in Carinhall [Goering's mansion] if he refused to testify before Hitler about the blackmail he was supposed to have levied. Gisevius alleged that the case, with its mistaken identity, had been on the Gestapo files since 1935, but that Goering only raised the matter when Hitler mentioned the possibility that Fritsch might be suitable to take over Blomberg's position. Goering was sufficiently uneasy at Nuremberg to send Gisevius threatening messages in an attempt to stop him saying too much about the Blomberg case. On the other hand, Meisinger, the man responsible for preparing the case against Fritsch, is said to have admitted he also faked evidence against Erna Gruhn, using her mother's dossier to do so, and that neither Hitler nor Goering knew of the matter in this form prepared for Heydrich until after Blomberg's wedding.

(Reprinted by permission of The Random House Group Ltd.)

Answer to question 4: A-grade candidate

(a) In the two years after Hitler and the Nazis came to power in 1933, Goering held various and numerous positions in the Nazi Party as indicated in Source 1, ranging from President of the Reichstag to Reich President for Aviation, Prussian Minister of the Interior and even Reich Forestry Commissioner and Controller of the Hunt. This lengthy list of positions would suggest that, at least in the early period of Nazi control, Goering had built up a great position of power as his roles covered most aspects of government; the military, policing, the economy, 'parliamentary' politics, and home affairs. It is also true that in this period Goering seemed at times to be ruthless and successful in carrying out these roles. For example, along with

Himmler, he was instrumental in the organisation of the Night of the Long Knives in 1934. However, despite these positions it has been argued that Goering was not as influential and powerful initially as this list would suggest. The nature of the positions, and the increasing power of other Nazis such as those mentioned in Source 1 — Ley, Himmler and Goebbels — would help suggest this as would the reference to disasters in 1933–34 in Source 4.

Source 2, however, does show how Goering gained a crucial position of substantial power. It is the speech from Hitler declaring that Goering was to be put in charge of the four-year plan. It details what powers he will have, 'to hear and to issue instructions to all authorities, including the Supreme Authorities'. Therefore we see that this position does truly give Goering great power over the German economy. Source 1 backs this up, as it states that this position 'provided a personal power base for him'. This was especially useful for him in the war, where his access to raw materials was vital for his control of the *Luftwaffe*, another position of power that, as Source 1 states, he managed to avoid losing. However, it has been suggested that he only held this position because Hitler felt he could control the economy through him. This is because Schacht, the previous economic minister, was against Hitler's ideas of autarky (self-sufficiency), whereas Goering would follow Hitler's orders. This would seem to suggest that Hitler gained influence, not Goering. There is much evidence that Goering was very submissive to his Führer and this could therefore be a valid reason for him being given this position. He had even stated, 'I have no conscience, Adolf Hitler is my conscience' and 'I follow no leadership but that of Adolf Hitler and of God'. However, Goering gained a great personal fortune from his part in the economy, not least from the Reichswerke, known as the 'Hermann Goering Steel Works'.

The idea that Goering had Hitler's support is echoed in Source 4, which further details why he was allowed the power detailed in Sources 1 and 2 and how he gained these positions. If Goering was as powerful as his list of offices would suggest, Sources 1 and 4 go some way to explaining why he was able to do this. Source 1 stresses the importance of the *Forschungsamt* — 'the one real asset he preserved.' Source 4 talks about the fact that Goering had great popular support from the press and the public at large, which the other conservatives never had and therefore 'under such circumstances there was no chance of dislodging Goering'. This could explain why he managed to gain positions, because he was popular and so his policies would gain support. The source goes on to describe how many leading Nazis were jealous of, and even hated, Goering. This again suggests he obviously was powerful, and had the support of the Führer. However, it goes on to explain how Goering reacted, calling Keitel and Lammers 'mere secretaries' because they tried to get between him and Hitler. This could explain why sometimes he did lose out because he made himself unpopular with key figures around Hitler. However, the source also states that 'he rode roughshod over them all, supported by an ever-growing circle of subordinate officials...'

However, there is also evidence, as Source 1 mentions, that Goering was not so successful. There were many examples of him losing positions and being overlooked for positions he may have thought were for him. Even though the source does show how some of his positions gave him power, it gives the example that his position as 'Minister of the Interior in Prussia had been eroded by the amalgamation of the Reich and Prussian Ministries under Frick'. It also talks about the 'monopoly of control over the police' which Himmler was building up and which he lost to Himmler in 1934. Another example is the fact that when he had helped remove Blomberg and Fritsch in 1938 he was not given the leadership of the army by Hitler, a position he fully expected to gain. This suggests that he was only given positions that Hitler could control him through, or that he thought Goering could handle. Therefore, the extent of his power is questionable.

Therefore, there are two issues, firstly, the extent to which Goering had power, and secondly how he gained this. Compared to people like Himmler, Goering did not have vast increasing power. Himmler showed a steady upward curve in power, whereas Goering's power increased and decreased unevenly, showing bursts of energy. He did have power because he had Hitler's support, he had the support of the press, and he did have many influential positions, some of which, such as control of the *Luftwaffe*, he kept until the end. However, he did lose out to many for other positions, and the support of Hitler, as Source 4 states, could explain why he lost certain positions and gained others, as Source 1 states. It seems in some ways Hitler gave him positions he could control him through, not necessarily to give him personal power. However, all three sources do agree that the positions did, to some extent, give Goering personal power, and considerable influence in the Third Reich.

> This is clearly a quality answer, if somewhat long. Sources and knowledge are used in the opening paragraph as they are throughout the essay, with focus maintained on both parts of the question. The response would be worth 9/10 marks.

(b) Throughout the Nazi regime Hitler was at the top of the power system, somewhat removed in stature from many others below him, all of whom shared similar levels of power and influence. The main people included here would be Goebbels, Goering, Himmler, Hess and Bormann, and also Ley and others. They constantly vied for the support of the Führer as well as trying to gain themselves power and personal influence. Source 2 talks about how easy it was for such individuals to manipulate Hitler. It talks about how 'the cunning men could gain more and more power'. Speer, who was one such himself, explains how Hitler was easily deceived by 'clever chess moves', and therefore this would have provided a good basis for the internal wrangling and power struggling of the powerful players. They knew that if they were subtle and cunning enough, they could gain the support of Hitler for what they wanted to do. This, therefore, provides a suggestion for why the schemes mentioned in the other sources occurred and why many were successful.

Source 1 is a useful illustration of how power was so easily shifted between the main players, as it describes the ups and downs in the power of Goering. It talks about how he gained positions and lost others, and therefore is useful for showing why it was so competitive within the party. For example, in 1933, Goering had much power, as Minister of the Interior for Prussia. This gave him policing powers. However, when Himmler started building up his SS state 'monopoly over police', Goering lost out and lost power. Therefore we can see how volatile the power system was, and therefore why there was so much deception and competition between Hitler's subordinates. Source 1 also goes on to explain how Himmler, Goebbels and Ley all 'combined party power with government office', whereas Goering 'held no party office which would allow him to compete'. This would suggest that Goering would have been thirsty to gain more positions, in order to compete with these three, and this is mirrored in Source 5, which gives the example of the 'Blomberg–Fritsch affair', in 1937–38. Although it is not conclusive that Goering was to blame for the downfall of Blomberg, it gives some evidence for the fact that he may have been, and also serves as an illustration of wrangling and deception used in order to gain power. After the Night of the Long Knives in 1934, Himmler was left to build up the SS state, whereas Goering was left with only the *Luftwaffe* and his intelligence network. Goering assumed that if Blomberg and Fritsch, who were the leaders of the army, were to be removed, he would be in line to become commander of the army as well as of the *Luftwaffe*. This shows again, as Source 1 suggests, how competitive the different members of the party were. Blomberg was removed because of scandalous stories brought to light about him, making, as Source 5 states, 'his position untenable'. The source then goes on to suggest that Fritsch was removed because it appeared he was next in line for Blomberg's position. Therefore the source suggests that Goering had a motive, and Gisevius, who provided evidence at the Nuremberg Trials, showed how Goering had been responsible. Therefore we see an example in Source 5 of how an individual removed others to gain the power he felt he needed, as mentioned in Source 1.

However, Source 4 does show Goering in a slightly different light, and shows that all his struggles for power, i.e. with Röhm, Himmler and then Blomberg and Fritsch, provided him with powerful positions, and even raised him to be seen as 'the Führer's second in command' — 'he could ignore many of the squabbles that went on around him'. This agrees with Source 2, which shows how Hitler provided him with the great power over the economy and 'the authority to issue legal decrees', etc.

Source 4 is a very clear explanation of the amount of struggling for power that went on, and also the fact that there was a lot of 'bitchiness' going on within the party, with members vying for power and trying to get 'one up' on someone else. Again, the source uses Goering's example as a basis for the argument. However, it looks at Goering's great personal support among the German public, which 'none of the other conservatives had'. It states that he had control of the press and 'under such circumstances there was no question of dislodging him'. The source then goes on to explain the rivalry within the party, how individuals such as Streicher, Hess and Rosenberg were so jealous of his power that they published stories about him and refused to allow photos that made him look good. Here we see clear examples of how there was great rivalry within the party. It also explains how Goering fought back with comments and rumours about other leaders such as Ribbentrop, Keitel and Lammers. This shows how there was a lot of struggling within the party to gain power, and jealousy towards those who had gained power.

However, the above would generally suggest that most of the power for people such as Himmler and Goering was gained through devious struggles, 'dishing the dirt' on other party members and manipulation of Hitler. Source 2, which was spoken by Hitler, suggests that the power struggles, internal wrangling and deceit which went on between the individual party members was to no avail. This source would seem to suggest that power was not completely gained by these struggles, because unless Hitler himself decreed so, individuals would not gain office. Therefore, the evidence of Source 2 would suggest that power was handed out by Hitler, and therefore the political system was marked by the internal power struggles beneath Hitler but not threatening him. There is obvious evidence from Sources 4 and 5 that there was much competition, but we can also see that it was not successful. For example, Goering did not gain the position of Blomberg after that power struggle, because Hitler did not feel he was up to the task. Therefore the struggle did not work, and Source 2 shows that Goering was given different positions, by Hitler himself.

Therefore, it is possible to suggest that Hitler really was completely in charge and all power was given to people by him, regardless of what deception went on below. Source 4 also mentions how Goering could not be removed as long as he had Hitler's support, and all the stories made up by others did not remove him from power. However, this does contradict the information in Source 3, that they realised how Hitler could be manipulated and therefore could gain position and power through controlling him. However, if this were true, how was it that Goering did not gain the position he expected in Source 5, but was given immense power over the economy, detailed in Source 2?

In conclusion it does seem that there was a great amount of rivalry and jealousy within the hierarchy of the Nazi regime, and that many schemes and deceptions were carried out in order for individuals to gain, or attempt to gain, positions of great power. It is probably also true that Hitler in some form was open to clever manipulation. However, the example of Goering in Sources 2 and 5 suggests that Hitler really was in charge of giving power and, despite the wrangling, the political system was only marked by constant struggle amongst Hitler's subordinates because many were not successful and it boiled down to Hitler's own decision. Hitler didn't want Goering in charge of the army, even though Goering had possibly removed Blomberg and Fritsch because he believed he would gain the position. However, as Source 2 states, Hitler did give him a position in the economy, which he felt Goering could do well. Therefore, it all seems to come down to Hitler. It is true that there were power struggles and in some cases these may have worked, e.g. the Night of the Long Knives gained Himmler much support. However, unless Hitler himself needed to gain from these schemes, it seemed always to come down to his final decision.

> This uses all the sources effectively, cross-referencing between them and linking them with 'own knowledge' to form a supported judgement. The essay could have been strengthened by some reference to the historiography surrounding this topic (covered in the Content Guidance section of this book). But this omission does not preclude a grade A, 16/20 marks, for this answer.

■ ■ ■

Answer to question 4: C-grade candidate

(a) Due to many attributes, Hitler gave him many powerful positions. Source 1 tells us of his being Minister of the Interior in Prussia, and hence the initial controller of the Gestapo. He also controlled the *Luftwaffe*, the German air force, and Hitler put him in charge of the four-year economic plan, where he had the authority to issue legal decrees. Doubtless, he gained a lot of power from these jobs.

However, there were problems. One was his own attitude to power. Source 4 describes his 'bemedalled appearance'. Goering took on several jobs, possibly too many, enjoying the status it gave him, although unable to cope with the workload. From most accounts he did not even attempt to. Another weakness was that he did not build up any 'monopoly of control', such as Himmler had over the SS, something Source 1 makes reference to. Because of this lack of specialisation, Himmler had been able to take power from him, when he convinced Hitler to transfer the Gestapo to him.

Unlike another of his rivals, Goebbels, Goering was not doing jobs for which he had flair. For the four-year economic plan, he didn't even have any economic training. Source 2 demonstrates the sheer weight of the task, but Goering took it on anyway.

The biggest problem Goering faced, though, was his dependence on Hitler. He enjoyed little support from the rest of the Nazi leadership. Source 4 says that he was 'increasingly isolated and distant'. Should Hitler lose faith in him, Goering would lose his power very quickly — he had no safety nets.

In conclusion, Goering did enjoy a lot of power in Nazi Germany, but there were limitations. He had no personal empire, like Goebbels' propaganda empire or Himmler's SS, and hence was entirely dependent on Hitler's whim. Apart from his ability to make Hitler trust in him, he did not have a specialised ability for any of his jobs, only obedience to Hitler, and therefore he was replaceable.

> Although own knowledge and the sources are used and there is an attempt to assess the extent of Goering's power, there is no real attempt to explain 'why'. This is therefore a partial answer and would only be awarded 5/10 marks.

(b) It is very difficult to tell how much the form Nazism took was the responsibility of Hitler or the result of the power battles among his subordinates. Hitler had the final say on all important matters, but he could be influenced by his subordinates, generally to their personal advantage.

Some of the struggles took place at a very high level, such as the Blomberg–Fritsch affair referred to in Source 5. As Source 5 shows, we cannot be entirely sure how involved Goering was in bringing down Blomberg and Fritsch, but he definitely behaved guiltily at the Nuremberg trials. The removal of Blomberg and Fritsch from their positions in the army allowed some significant changes.

Similarly the Night of the Long Knives was another occasion where the power struggles between Hitler's subordinates might have changed the political system of the Third Reich in a way that Hitler had not planned. It appears that it was Goering and Himmler, wanting to remove a rival, who first convinced Hitler that a 'Röhm putsch' was imminent, and then convinced him to have Röhm shot. Hitler had been dithering over this point. The removal of Röhm changed the face of Nazism. It became more 'respectable' to the Germans, willing to collude with the older German powers through losing Röhm's revolutionary fervour and attitudes.

Source 3 supports this interpretation of the struggles having profound effects, saying that Hitler 'could be swayed'. There is still no doubt that he had the final say, but he might not have been altogether consistent in organising Nazism the way he wanted because of being influenced by others.

The way certain Nazi institutions developed was also a result of power struggles between subordinate Nazis, and was dependent on their personalities. Source 1 talks about Goering losing his control of the Prussian police force to Himmler. Had it not been for Himmler's success here against his rivals, the Third Reich would not have been such a formidable police state.

Hitler did not appear to have the interest to involve himself deeply in the general day-to-day running of the Nazi state. From all accounts, he spent very little time actually working, and a lot more time watching films and discussing architecture. Therefore, it was mainly left up to his subordinates, and the result of their struggles would determine the events.

This argument for the Nazi system being entirely the result of subordinates' struggles cannot be entirely agreed with, however. Source 2 shows that Hitler did give orders, in fact he planned out over a span of years how Nazism should unfold. Add to this the evidence of his book, *Mein Kampf*, with its definite outline of goals and objectives for the Nazi state, and you get a different idea. His subordinates were following the orders he gave them.

In the Blomberg–Fritsch affair, Goering was involved, but he was following a general hint Hitler had given him. Hitler had said that he intended to 'light a fire' under Blomberg and Fritsch. One could interpret this event as Hitler manipulating Goering to do Hitler's dirty work for him. Goering didn't even particularly benefit from the outcome.

In the Night of the Long Knives again, Goering and Himmler might simply have told Hitler what he wanted to hear. Hitler needed a good excuse to get rid of Röhm because he was upsetting the army. Hitler needed the army to support him.

Furthermore, Hitler's habit of sometimes putting two different groups of people on the same job ensured that they competed against each other rather than him. He could be said to have encouraged fights between his subordinates himself, well knowing the effects.

Saying that struggle between the subordinates was all-important does not accord entirely with Source 4 either. Source 4 implies that the top Nazis did not necessarily fight often.

A lot of the struggles amongst the more minor Nazis had very little effect on what happened.

In conclusion, one has to decide somewhere between the two arguments. Ian Kershaw's explanation of 'working towards the Führer' seems to fit.

Hitler gave the orders, giving his subordinates a direction to follow. He then left them to it, checking at the end that they had done what he wanted. This left his orders open to interpretation, and his subordinates would argue amongst themselves. However, as he would fire people who got it wrong, people would do their best.

e The obvious defect here is the tendency to want to answer another, if related, question on Hitler's power and the structuralist/intentionalist debate. There is some (if inadequate) use of the sources and some accurate knowledge, but a distinctly shaky focus. The use of paragraphs is inappropriate, and it is important to strive for quality of communication. The candidate would earn half the marks available, 10/20.

Question 5

(a) Using your own knowledge and Sources 1, 3 and 4, assess the impact of the Nazi regime on living standards in the years 1933–39. (10 marks)

(b) Using your own knowledge and all the sources, assess the popularity of the Nazi regime in the years 1933–39. (20 marks)

Source 1: *From* Good Times, Bad Times: Memories of the Third Reich, U. Herbert, 1983

As late as 1951 almost half of those citizens of the Federal Republic of Germany questioned in a public opinion survey described the period between 1933 and 1939 as the one in which things had gone best for Germany.

All 'politics' aside, for a large part of the population the image of National Socialism was characterised principally not by terror, mass murder and war but by reduction of unemployment, economic boom, tranquility and order. In 1949 the Institut für Demoskopie (Public Opinion Institute) summarised the result of its survey of the 'Consequences of National Socialism'. There was 'no more talk of German rebirth or of racial awakening among the population; these bits of Third Reich décor are antiquated, worn out, finished'. On the other hand, memories of the 'positive' aspects of National Socialism were still as fresh as ever:

> The guaranteed pay packet, order, KdF [*Kraft durch Freude*, Stength through Joy, the National Socialist leisure organisation] and the smooth running of the political machinery...Thus 'National Socialism' makes them think merely of work, adequate nourishment, KdF and the absence of 'disarray' in political life.

The result of these post-war opinion surveys into the German people's memories of Nazism correspond at many points to the findings of a large oral-history project that has been carried out for the past four years at the universities of Essen and Hagen under the direction of Lütz Niethammer: Life History and Social Culture in the Ruhr, 1930–1960.

Source 2: *From* The Nazi Seizure of Power: The Experiences of a Single German Town, W. S. Allen, 1965

Those who had the time and inclination to assess the nature of Nazism, by 1935, could set up a balance sheet. On the one hand, Nazism had apparently ended the depression, initiated an economic revival, beautified the town, provided vigorous and efficient leadership, and increased Northeim's economic assets. On the other hand, it had vitiated and regimented social life, introduced a system of terror and authoritarianism, attacked the churches, forced Northeimers to participate in a constant round of dulling and ritualistic propaganda events, and tied the fortunes of the town to the personal whims and dubious personality of Ernst Girmann. Obviously the balance did not resolve itself into a simple equation.

By 1935 most Northeimers were again unsure about Nazism. It is extremely hard to say what the results of a free election might have been. The odds are that in the minds of most Northeimers the bad outweighed the good. Given the chance, they probably would have voted to end or alter the Nazi regime. But long before 1935 the decision had been fixed.

Source 3: *Statistics of recovery in Germany 1933–38 from R. J. Overy,* The Nazi Economic Recovery

	1928	1932	1933	1934	1935	1936	1937	1938
GNP (Reichsmarks bn)	89.5	71.9	73.7	83.7	92.3	101.2	114.2	126.2
Unemployment (m)	1.4	5.6	4.8	2.7	2.2	1.6	0.9	0.4

Source 4: *Consumption in working-class families from R. J. Overy,* The Nazi Economic Recovery

	1927	1937	% change
Rye bread (kg)	262.9	316.1	+20.2
Wheat bread (kg)	55.2	30.8	−44.2
Meat and meat products (kg)	133.7	109.2	−18.3
Bacon (kg)	9.5	8.5	−10.5
Milk (ltr)	427.8	367.2	−14.2
Eggs (no.)	404.0	237.0	−41.3
Fish (kg)	21.8	20.4	−6.4
Vegetables (kg)	117.2	109.6	−6.5
Potatoes (kg)	499.5	519.8	+4.1
Sugar (kg)	47.2	45.0	−4.7
Tropical fruit (kg)	9.7	6.1	−37.1
Beer (ltr)	76.5	31.6	−58.7

Source 5: *From* The Past is Myself, *Christabel Bielenberg, an opponent of the Nazi regime*

What had Hitler provided which seemed to satisfy so many and persuaded them so easily to relinquish their freedom and to turn aside from the still small voice of their conscience? I was ignorant at the time, but later I felt I could venture a guess. Hitler understood his Germans well, or maybe he just chanced his luck with human nature. There was a titbit for all in his political stewpot. Work for the unemployed, an army for the generals, a phoney religion for the gullible, a loud, insistent and not unheeded voice in international affairs for those who still smarted under the indignity of a lost war: there were also detention camps and carefully broadcast hints of what might be in store for anyone who had the temerity to enquire into his methods too closely, let alone openly disapprove of them. He made every move through a smoke screen of legality and of propriety.

(This extract from *The Past is Myself*, first published by Chatto and Windus Ltd, 1968, now published by Corgi, © Christabel Bielenberg, is reproduced by kind permission of the author.)

Answer to question 5: A-grade candidate

(a) The Nazi regime is always remembered, as Source 1 states, for the Holocaust, the persecution of Jews and other enemies and the way it treated those it occupied during the war. However, in Germany itself, the period of 1933–39, by all accounts, was of a considerably higher standard than previous periods had been. As long as you were not regarded as an enemy of the regime, i.e. you weren't a Communist, or socialist, or Jewish, you would have probably benefited, as many Germans did, from the social and economic policies of Nazism.

The Weimar Period, pre-1933, had caused many economic problems in Germany. Despite the 'golden age', the economic crisis (which resulted in hyperinflation in 1923) and the Wall Street Crash in 1929 had caused serious problems for the German economy. This resulted in poorer standards of living and less food, especially in the rural areas. The statistics in Source 3 show how the economic nature of Germany changed as a result of these problems and then as a result of the Nazi rise to power. In 1928, before the economic crisis, we see the GNP at a quite high 89.5 billion Reichsmarks. However, this drops dramatically by 1932. Then, when the Nazis come into power, we see a steady increase, until in 1938 it is 126.2 billion Reichsmarks, much higher than even before the crisis. There is a similar pattern in the figures for employment. The numbers in work recovered after the crisis, and raised employment to new highs. This statistical evidence would back up the information in Source 1. The source states that many people believed that 'the period between 1933 and 1939 [was] one in which things had gone best for Germany'. We can see how the statistics provide evidence for the 'economic boom' that 'characterised' national socialism. People were earning more, and more people were working. Therefore Sources 1 and 3 would confirm that National Socialism was very economically beneficial to Germany, and this would suggest that it had also a beneficial effect on living standards.

Source 1 also talks about the way the actual policies and schemes of the party improved life for people in Germany. The source gives the example of *Kraft durch Freude*, or 'strength through joy'. This party organisation arranged holidays and cultural visits for German workers and their families. It is this that the source states people remembered about the regime; 'on the other hand, memories of the positive aspects of national socialism were still fresh as ever'. This shows that through such schemes Nazism must have benefited the lives of the people. The source also talks about unemployment being lower, as the statistics in Source 3 again confirm. All these factors would suggest Nazism was positive and that was how people remembered it.

However, Source 1 talks about 'adequate nourishment', and this would conflict with statistical evidence in Source 4. Source 4 shows the consumption of certain foodstuffs in 1927 and also in 1937, i.e. under Nazism. This shows that for many foods, consumption went down dramatically, and the decreases were much greater than the increases. This would suggest that there was less food available, and therefore maybe not 'adequate consumption' as Source 1 states. For example, although rye bread increased in consumption, it only did so by 20.2%, whereas wheat bread decreased by 44.2%, over twice the increase. This could have been due to Hitler's policy of autarky. He wanted Germany to be self-sufficient, to provide for itself, and so some items, such as wheat, may not have been readily available. Therefore, some of the policies may not have benefited living standards but had a negative effect, such as this example of economic policy meaning less food availability.

Therefore we see a conflict between the sources. Sources 1 and 3 seem to suggest that living standards had improved under National Socialism, whereas Source 4 would suggest that maybe Nazism had a negative effect in many areas of consumption, through some of Hitler's own policies, in which he wanted Germany to be autonomous and provide for itself. However, despite the decline in diet for many Germans, there were compensations in the spread of radio and more frequent visits to the cinema.

> This is a straightforward A-grade response worth 8/10 marks, using the appropriate data from the sources, which is cross-referenced and blended with 'own knowledge'.

(b) The popularity of a terroristic regime such as that of the Nazis can be questioned. When such violence and terror is used alongside other policies, it is always possible that the support of the people for a certain cause is not necessarily a measure of its actual popularity, but of its success in coercing people into supporting them. However, despite the widespread use of intimidation, indicated in Source 5, there is much evidence that the regime was popular, as Source 2 indicates.

The start of Source 2 sums up some of the positive points of the regime, reflecting the statistical evidence in Source 3 and also the memories of people as reported in Source 1. However, this source also suggests that the regime may not have been so popular, therefore we see two clear sides of the argument outlined in this source.

question

There were positive sides of the regime that made National Socialism popular, but also negative points.

Sources 1 and 3 would suggest that living standards had improved dramatically under the Nazi regime from what they were under Weimar. This marked difference would obviously have made the Nazi Party more popular. The statistics in Source 3 show how unemployment dropped during the Nazi period, from 5.6% in 1932 to only 0.4% in 1937, even lower than 1928, before the economic crisis. The recovery from the economic crisis had been cleverly planned by the government, to improve conditions and also gain popularity through doing this. They strove to improve the number of jobs, lower unemployment and aid industry by directly investing funds for improvement, reducing the taxes paid by farmers, small businesses and big industry, and also centralised the regulation of prices, wages and banking. The statistics in Source 3 obviously show that this recovery plan had worked, as does Source 1. Source 1 details the results of an opinion poll taken after the regime of German people and their memories and views of Nazism. The economic plan is mirrored here, as people stated they remembered positively 'the guaranteed pay packet...the work, adequate nourishment'. The fact that, even after Nazism had collapsed and Germany had lost another war, this was what people remembered, suggests that the regime had been popular for the way it had handled the economy, and improved living and working standards. Source 2 also mentions the benefits of the regime, 'economic revival...increased Northeim's economic assets'. All three sources would suggest that the 'economic boom' of the period made at least this aspect of the regime popular amongst the German masses.

Economic advantages were not the only benefits that people gained from Nazism. There were many social activities organised by the party, all with a political message, but which were obviously popular and would have made the party quite popular too. Source 1 specifically mentions 'strength through joy', an organisation which provided holidays and cultural visits for German workers and their families. There were also other movements, such as the Hitler Youth, and the BdM, which were the Nazi youth organisations for males and females respectively. They provided entertainment and activities for children, designed to improve the new Aryan race, the future of Germany. Such organisations would have increased popularity as they provided something else rather than just politics, and were also well attended. This idea fits in with Source 5, which talks about there being 'a titbit for all in the political stewpot' — meaning Nazism provided something for everyone. The source talks about there being 'work for the unemployed' (again mirroring the theme in Sources 1, 2 and 3) and a voice 'for those who still smarted under the indignity of a lost war' and 'an army for the generals'. This source would therefore suggest that Nazism had widespread popularity because it had something for everyone, including the economic advantages shown in the other sources, and the social activities it provided, as with the KdF, mentioned in Source 1. Source 5 states that this was how Hitler was able to persuade so many 'to relinquish their freedom'.

However, Sources 2 and 5 are similar in that they also give insight into the other side of the argument, that Nazism maybe was not so popular as the other sources might suggest. Firstly, they both suggest that terror played an important role in making people support the party, and therefore popularity was a result of violent coercion, or threats of violence. Source 5 mentions the positive aspects, but goes on to say 'and there were also the detention camps and carefully broadcast hints of what might be in store for anyone who had the temerity to enquire into his methods too closely, let alone openly disapprove of them'. This is mirrored in Source 2, which talks about the 'system of terror and authoritarianism' and the way people were 'forced...to participate'. These would suggest that support and popularity may have been less than genuine, and more likely coerced through fear.

Source 2 suggests quite clearly that at least in Northeim, by 1935 the popularity of the party was waning. It actually suggests that if 'free elections' were held again (all other parties had been banned by this point), the Nazis might not win, and that 'most Northeimers were again unsure about Nazism'. It suggests the reason for this is that they had become fed up with being forced to attend endless propaganda rallies (in some areas members had to prove they had actually attended events, because fewer and fewer people were attending). The attacks on churches were not popular, and in Northeim, the Gauleiter, the local party leader, was obviously not popular. The second part of this source shows quite clearly how people were becoming bored and disillusioned with the party; it even states that for the majority 'the bad outweighed the good' in terms of the Nazi regime. This apathy, especially towards the endless propaganda, was widespread. People would arrive at the cinema late on purpose to miss the propaganda newsreel and only see the film. The fact that a law had to be passed in 1937 calling for cinema doors to be locked and latecomers turned away shows how widespread the problem had become. As well, there is the obvious problem about the way that enemies were treated, for example the actions of the SS and Gestapo. This, for some Germans, would have made the party unpopular. The main message of Source 2 is that although there were good economic points, the party support was waning by 1935 and it was not as popular as it seemed.

Source 4 would even suggest that the economic advantages were not as great as the statistics and information in 1, 2 and 3 would suggest. It shows how consumption of many foodstuffs had decreased dramatically between 1927 (pre-Nazis) and 1937. This would suggest that under Nazism some foods were less available. This may have been due to Hitler's policy of autarky, self-sufficiency. He wanted Germany to provide for itself, and therefore some foods may have become more scarce. This contradicts the 'adequate nourishment' which Source 1 describes, suggesting that under Nazism there was actually a more limited supply of food, in amount and variety. This would mean that surely they were less popular regarding living standards than the other sources suggest.

Therefore we can see clearly that there are two arguments. Firstly, that the regime was very popular, because living standards had improved and people were working. This surely would have given them a lot of popularity. The party was also seen to be 'doing something' for the people, for example with 'strength through joy', which would also have gained them popularity. However, we see clearly in Source 2 that at least in some places people were becoming fed up with the endless propaganda and the way enemies were treated. It seems that at least to a certain extent there is evidence to suggest Nazism wasn't popular, or at least by the end of this pre-war period was a lot less popular than it had been in 1933. Terror and fear may have played a large role in keeping up popularity. However, the fact that Source 1 was written after the terrible atrocities of the Holocaust had come to light, and Germany had been defeated, shows how people had positive memories, and would suggest that the party had been genuinely popular. This may have been mainly in terms of economic recovery, but we do see how people had positive memories. Therefore, there seems to be no clear answer. In some respects the party was popular, but in others people were bored and fed up, and had to be coerced into supporting, possibly with terror.

e Again this is a good, direct response which uses the evidence provided very well. It would have been strengthened still further by a discussion of the nature of evidence needed to answer a question like this. The reliability of Source 5 could be raised, and some reference made to the SOPADE reports and those of the SD, both of which sought to assess, for different motives, the popularity of the Nazi regime. The candidate would be awarded 17/20 marks.

Answer to question 5: C-grade candidate

(a) After the distress and insecurity of the Weimar years, especially the two economic crashes, the new order and organisation that Hitler's regime brought appears to have been welcomed by many in Germany. But did it manage to raise living standards?

One of the major problems the Nazis had to deal with was rising unemployment. As Source 3 shows us, this was something they managed to sort out, as the number of unemployed dropped steadily from 1933 onwards. There was a 'guaranteed pay packet', Source 1 tells us.

This economic recovery had a basis in government workplans, the building of the Autobahns being one example. The unemployed were conscripted into labour which they did not necessarily want to do. Some jobs were 'opened up' by the removal of women and Jews from jobs.

So the economic recovery might not have been stable, but it lasted during 1933–39, the conscripted workers received food and shelter, and the loss of women's and Jews' jobs only affected a minority. In monetary terms the situation had improved, but was there anything to buy?

Edexcel Unit 6

Source 1 also tells us of 'adequate nourishment'. Looking at Source 4, the idea of an improvement in food seems contradicted.

It appears that as far as food was concerned living standards dropped somewhat, but at least steady jobs meant fewer people went hungry.

The *Kraft durch Freude* organisation mentioned in Source 1 was important in showing an improvement in living standards at a certain level. It ensured that culture and entertainment was available to everyone, something which had never been done before. The health of the nation's children improved too, with the organised exercise of the Hitler Youth and the League of German Maidens.

In conclusion, due to an improving economic situation, and more interference with people's leisure time, the Nazis improved the living standards of the majority of the population during these years. The foundations were unstable, but this did not yet matter.

> This is a basic, rather source-based answer which would be awarded 5/10 marks. The major points are identified, but the statistical data in Sources 3 and 4 are used only in outline, and some relevant material in Source 1 is ignored.

(b) The end of the Nazi regime came only with the end of the Second World War. It must have been either their popularity or their ability to clamp down on opposition which kept them in power. As there was no concerted attempt to get rid of Hitler until as late as 1944 by the army generals, we must conclude that their strength had some basis in popularity. But how popular were they?

The Nazis had been elected with a big proportion of the vote in 1933 to solve the problems that the previous Weimar government had been unable to deal with: the weak state of the German economy, the rising unemployment, the unstable governments.

The Nazis had basically been given a mandate to sort out the economic situation. Effecting this should have given them popularity, but their other policies need to be taken into consideration too.

Source 3 shows that they were successful in bringing about economic recovery; GNP increased steadily and unemployment fell rapidly. Sources 1, 2 and 3 all agree that this aspect of the regime was popular.

The second thing which the Nazis sorted out was something only Source 1 touches upon positively. They restored 'tranquility and order' in the streets and in political life. Source 2 interprets this as 'a system of terror and authoritarianism' and Source 5 says that the Germans relinquished 'their freedom'. The matter under discussion here is the imposition of a police, one-party state. The attitudes of Sources 2 and 5 are indignant, but this is to be expected from non-Nazis writing after the event. However both sources portray this as something the Germans were willing to accept in return for economic stability. In fact the 'terror' was targeted only at minority, opposition groups in Germany, such as the left wing, the Jews, and homosexuals, not the majority of the Germans. The high level of collaboration that there was between the Germans and the Gestapo, volunteering information on neighbours and acquaintances, implies that the Gestapo were quite popular, although perhaps that is not the right word. At any rate the hostility towards them was limited.

One could say that the support was superficial, induced by fear, but Source 1, a poll taken in 1951, shows that for almost half the population the Nazis were popular.

The third main thing the Nazis brought was propaganda, the tool to increase their popularity. This was greeted with irritation in some areas. Source 2 tells us that in Northeim the residents became fed up at being forced to participate in 'dulling and ritualistic propaganda events', but these marches and talks were not the only form of propaganda. It was much more insidious and appeared successful. In Nazi Germany, propaganda was about trying to sell a set of beliefs and a lifestyle to people. To get people on their side, the Nazis organised popular activities during which they could slowly get across their propaganda. Organising this was *Kraft durch Freude*, the Nazi leisure organisation, recalled as one of the 'positive aspects' in Source 1. Nazism is described by Source 5 as 'a phoney religion for the gullible'.

Another thing the Nazis managed to give to people was a sense of national pride. Source 5 emphasises this. They had an army again and importance in the international arena. This cannot be underestimated as a source of popularity for the Nazis after the humiliation the Germans had suffered under the Treaty of Versailles and the subsequent Weimar period.

In conclusion, during the period 1933–39, the Nazis were generally popular. This was based on their success at improving the economic situation, and their own attempts to make themselves liked.

They did have their opponents, but these were not powerful. They were for the most part grumblers who were not prepared to act.

> *e* There is focus on the question here and all the sources are used to some degree, sometimes cross-referenced. There is even some reference to source utility, with use made of the attribution of Source 5. However, the 'own knowledge' is strictly limited and confined to two sections into which the source material is not allowed to intrude. There are three, admittedly short, paragraphs before the mention of a source. It is important to stress that it is the integration of sources and knowledge that is looked for. Overall this response would be worth 10/20 marks.